VEGAN ASIAN COOKBOOK

The Ultimate Guide to Plant-Based Asian Cooking for Every Kitchen

BELINDA K. MARROW

Copyright © 2024 By BELINDA K. MARROW. All rights reserved worldwide.

No part of this book may be reproduced or transmitted in any form or by any means, electronic or mechanical, including photocopying, recording, or by any information storage and retrieval system, without written permission from the publisher, except for the inclusion of brief quotations in a review.

Warning-Disclaimer:

The purpose of this book is to educate and entertain. The author or publisher does not guarantee that anyone following the techniques, suggestions, tips, ideas, or strategies will become successful. The author and publisher shall have neither liability nor responsibility to anyone with respect to any loss or damage caused, or alleged to be caused, directly or indirectly, by the information contained in this book.

This copyright notice and disclaimer apply to the entirety of the book and its contents, whether in print or electronic form, and extend to all future editions or revisions of the book. Unauthorized use or reproduction of this book or its contents is strictly prohibited and may result in legal action.

TABLE OF CONTENTS

INTRODUCTION TO VEGAN ASIAN CUISINE 7
HISTORY AND CULTURAL SIGNIFICANCE 8
COMMONLY USED INGREDIENTS AND COOKING TECHNIQUES 9
TIPS FOR SUCCESSFUL VEGAN ASIAN COOKING 11

APPETIZERS AND SMALL BITES 13

Fresh and Crispy Vegetable Spring Rolls 13
Edamame Dumplings with Soy-Ginger Dipping Sauce 13
Crispy Tofu Bites with Spicy Peanut Sauce 14
Refreshing Vietnamese Fresh Rolls with Peanut Dipping Sauce 15
Tangy Mango Salad Rolls with Lime Dipping Sauce 16
Vegetable Samosas 17
Baked Veggie Pot Stickers 17
Avocado Cucumber Rolls 18
Crispy Cauliflower Wings 19
Vegetable Tempura 19
Sweet Chili Tofu Bites 20
Vegan Shumai Dumplings 20
Baked Veggie Samosa Bites 21
Vegan Scallion Pancakes 22
Crispy Vegetable Fritters 22

SOUPS AND BROTHS 24

Vegan Hot and Sour Soup 24
Miso Soup 25
Vegetable Wonton Soup 25
Thai Coconut Soup 26
Vietnamese Pho 27
VegetableLaksa 28
Vegan Ramen 29
Spicy Kimchi Soup 29
Vegan Congee 30
Vegetable Dumpling Soup 31

Mushroom Miso Soup 31

Vegetable Tom Kha Soup 32

Vegan Mulligatawny Soup 33

Vegan Pho Broth 34

Vegetable Soybean Soup 35

SALADS AND SIDE DISHES 36

Vegan Sushi Salad 36

Thai Mango Salad 36

Chinese Cucumber Salad 37

Korean Bulgogi Lettuce Wraps 38

Vietnamese Noodle Salad 39

Japanese Potato Salad 40

Vegan Egg Roll in a Bowl 40

Spicy Cucumber Salad 41

Vegetable Pad Thai Salad 42

Vegan Japchae Noodles 43

Asian Slaw 44

Vegan Sticky Rice 45

Steamed Baby Bok Choy 45

Vegan Kimchi 46

Baked Tofu Teriyaki Bites 47

RICE AND NOODLE DISHES 49

Vegan Pad Thai 49

Vegetable Lo Mein 50

Vegan Fried Rice 51

Vegan Chow Mein 52

Vegan Pho with Rice Noodles 53

Vegetable Yakisoba 54

Vegan Pad See Ew 55

Vegetable Singapore Noodles 56

Vegan Japchae 57

Vegan Drunken Noodles 58

Vegan Laksa 59

Vegetable Chow Fun 60

Vegan Kake Soba 61

Vegetable Bibimbap 62

Vegan Pad Kee Mao 63

STIR-FRIES AND CURRIES 65

Vegan Thai Red Curry 65

Vegetable Chop Suey 66

Vegan Massaman Curry 66

Kung Pao Vegetables 67

Vegan Thai Green Curry 68

Vegetable Pad Prik King 69

Vegan Japanese Curry 69

Vegetable Cashew Stir-Fry 70

Vegan Penang Curry 71

Tofu and Vegetable Stir-Fry 72

Vegan Rendang Curry 73

Vegetable Teriyaki Stir-Fry 73

Vegan Yellow Curry 74

Szechuan Tofu and Vegetable Stir-Fry 75

Vegan Coconut Curry 76

TOFU AND MEAT ALTERNATIVES 77

Crispy Baked Tofu 77

Vegan "Beef" and Broccoli 77

Vegan Mapo Tofu 78

Vegan "Chicken" Teriyaki 79

Vegetable Tofu Lettuce Wraps 80

Vegan Lemongrass "Chicken" 81

Vegan BBQ "Pork" Bao Buns 81

Sesame Crusted Tofu 82

Vegan Mongolian "Beef" 83

Vegan Tempeh Rendang 83

Vegan Seitan Satay 84

Vegan "Chicken" Tikka Masala 85

Tofu Katsu Curry 86

Vegan "Beef" Pho 87

Vegan "Chicken" Larb 88

DESSERTS AND SWEET TREATS 89

Vegan Mango Sticky Rice 89

Coconut Tapioca Pudding 89

Vegan Red Bean Soup 90

Lychee Sorbet 90

Vegan Mochi Ice Cream 91

Vegan Thai Tea Popsicles 92

Vegan Matcha Cake 92

Coconut Pandan Waffles 93

Vegan Black Sesame Soup 94

Vegan Green Tea Cheesecake 94

Pineapple Upside Down Cake 95

Vegan Sesame Balls 96

Vegan Mooncakes 96

Vegan Banana Fritters 97

Tropical Fruit Spring Rolls 98

BEVERAGES AND SMOOTHIES 99

Vegan Thai Iced Tea 99

Vegan Thai Iced Coffee 99

Vegan Bubble Tea 100

Tropical Smoothie 100

Dragonfruit Lemonade 101

Vegan Horchata 101

Vegan Taro Milk Tea 102

Vegan Soy Milk 103

Vegan Matcha Latte 103

Vegan Vietnamese Coffee 104

Coconut Lime Cooler 105

Vegan Turmeric Latte 105

Vegan Ginger Beer 106

Vegan Lassi 107
Vegan Salted Lemon Soda 107

BASICS AND ESSENTIALS 109

Vegan Fish Sauce 109
Vegan Oyster Sauce 109
Vegan Hoisin Sauce 110
Homemade Tofu 111
Vegan Chicken Stock 112
Vegan Beef Stock 112
Vegan Dashi 113
Vegan Kimchi 114
Vegan Sriracha 115
Vegan Sweet Chili Sauce 115
Vegan Peanut Sauce 116
Vegan Thai Curry Paste 117
Vegan Ponzu 118
Vegan Teriyaki Sauce 118
Vegan Gochujang 119

CONCLUSION 121

INTRODUCTION TO VEGAN ASIAN CUISINE

Vegan Asian cuisine offers a tantalizing array of flavors, textures, and cultural diversity, showcasing the rich culinary heritage of the continent while embracing plant-based ingredients. Rooted in traditions that span centuries, vegan Asian cuisine seamlessly blends aromatic spices, fresh produce, and innovative cooking techniques to create dishes that are both delicious and nourishing.

At the heart of vegan Asian cuisine lies a deep reverence for nature and a holistic approach to food. Drawing inspiration from Buddhist principles of compassion and non-violence, many Asian cultures have long embraced plant-based diets as a means of promoting harmony with the environment and living beings. This ethical foundation underpins the philosophy behind vegan Asian cuisine, elevating it beyond mere culinary practice to a lifestyle rooted in mindfulness and sustainability.

One of the defining characteristics of vegan Asian cuisine is its emphasis on fresh, seasonal ingredients. From the verdant rice paddies of Southeast Asia to the bustling markets of India, a bounty of fruits, vegetables, legumes, and grains form the cornerstone of plant-based meals. By celebrating the diversity of local produce, vegan Asian chefs are able to create dishes that are not only flavorful but also deeply nourishing, reflecting the vibrant tapestry of the region's culinary landscape.

In addition to its focus on fresh ingredients, vegan Asian cuisine is renowned for its bold and intricate flavors. Drawing on a vast repertoire of herbs, spices, and condiments, chefs artfully balance sweet, sour, salty, and spicy notes to create dishes that are as complex as they are satisfying. Whether it's the fiery heat of Sichuan peppers in Chinese cuisine or the aromatic blend of lemongrass and galangal in Thai cooking, vegan Asian dishes tantalize the taste buds with their depth of flavor and culinary finesse.

Moreover, vegan Asian cuisine is characterized by its versatility and adaptability. From street food stalls to fine dining establishments, plant-based options abound, catering to a diverse range of tastes and dietary preferences. Whether you're craving the comforting warmth of a steaming bowl of Japanese miso soup or the fiery kick of Korean kimchi, vegan Asian cuisine offers something for everyone, inviting diners to explore new flavors and culinary experiences.

Beyond its culinary appeal, vegan Asian cuisine also carries profound cultural significance, serving as a testament to the region's rich history and heritage. From the time-honored rituals of tea ceremonies in China to the elaborate feasts of Indian weddings, food plays a central role in Asian culture, serving as a vehicle for communal bonding and celebration. By embracing plant-based ingredients, vegan Asian cuisine honors this tradition while also adapting to the evolving tastes and values of modern society.

In conclusion, vegan Asian cuisine offers a harmonious fusion of flavors, ethics, and cultural heritage, inviting diners on a journey of culinary discovery and exploration. With its emphasis on fresh, seasonal ingredients, bold flavors, and cultural diversity, vegan Asian cuisine embodies the timeless principles of compassion, sustainability, and mindfulness, making it not just a meal, but a holistic and enriching experience for both the palate and the soul.

HISTORY AND CULTURAL SIGNIFICANCE

Throughout history, Asian cuisine has evolved in tandem with the diverse cultures and traditions of the continent, shaping both the culinary landscape and the cultural identity of its people. From the ancient civilizations of China and India to the bustling metropolises of Japan and South Korea, food has always occupied a central place in Asian culture, serving as a means of nourishment, celebration, and communal bonding.

The roots of Asian cuisine can be traced back thousands of years, with each region boasting its own unique culinary traditions and techniques. In China, for example, the invention of various cooking methods such as stir-frying, steaming, and braising revolutionized the way food was prepared and consumed, laying the foundation for what would later become one of the world's most influential cuisines. Similarly, the introduction of rice cultivation in India transformed the dietary habits of its people, giving rise to a rich tapestry of flavors and spices that continue to define Indian cuisine to this day.

As Asian societies evolved and interacted with one another, culinary traditions were exchanged, adapted, and refined, leading to the emergence of new and hybrid cuisines. The Silk Road, for instance, facilitated the exchange of goods and ideas between East and West, resulting in the fusion of flavors and ingredients from disparate regions. Spices such as cinnamon, cloves, and ginger, which were once considered luxuries in Europe, became integral components of Asian cuisine, imbuing dishes with exotic aromas and flavors.

Furthermore, the spread of Buddhism across Asia played a pivotal role in shaping the region's culinary landscape, particularly in regards to vegetarianism. As Buddhist monks traveled from India to China, Japan, and beyond, they brought with them a philosophy of compassion and non-violence that advocated for the abstention from meat consumption. This ethos resonated with many Asian cultures, leading to the development of a wide array of plant-based dishes that continue to be enjoyed today.

In addition to its historical roots, Asian cuisine also carries profound cultural significance, serving as a tangible expression of identity, heritage, and social hierarchy. In Japan, for example, the elaborate rituals of kaiseki cuisine reflect the country's reverence for nature and the changing seasons, while also showcasing the skill and artistry of its chefs. Similarly, the intricately spiced curries of India are not only a testament to the country's cultural diversity but also a symbol of hospitality and generosity.

Moreover, food plays a central role in many of Asia's religious and social traditions, serving as a conduit for spiritual communion and social cohesion. In China, the Lunar New Year is celebrated with elaborate feasts symbolizing prosperity and abundance, while in South Korea, the ritual of sharing a meal with family and friends, known as "jeong," is considered essential for maintaining harmonious relationships.

In conclusion, the history and cultural significance of Asian cuisine are deeply intertwined with the rich tapestry of traditions, beliefs, and values that define the continent. From its ancient origins to its modern-day manifestations, Asian cuisine reflects the diverse influences and dynamic interactions that have shaped the region's culinary heritage. By celebrating the past while also embracing the present, Asian cuisine continues to evolve, adapt, and inspire, serving as a testament to the enduring power of food to unite, nourish, and enrich the human experience.

COMMONLY USED INGREDIENTS AND COOKING TECHNIQUES

Asian cuisine is renowned for its vibrant flavors, aromatic spices, and innovative cooking techniques, which are made possible by a diverse array of commonly used ingredients. From fragrant herbs and spices to umami-rich sauces and condiments, these ingredients form the building blocks of countless Asian dishes, lending them their distinctive taste and character.

One of the most ubiquitous ingredients in Asian cuisine is rice, which serves as a staple food source for billions of people across the continent. Whether it's the fragrant jasmine rice of Thailand, the sticky sushi rice of Japan, or the long-grain basmati rice of India, rice is a versatile ingredient that can be steamed, fried, or boiled to accompany a wide variety of dishes.

Another essential component of Asian cuisine is noodles, which come in countless shapes, sizes, and textures, from thin and delicate rice noodles to thick and chewy wheat noodles. Noodles are a staple in many Asian cuisines, where they are used in soups, stir-fries, and cold salads, offering a hearty and satisfying base for a wide range of dishes.

In addition to rice and noodles, Asian cuisine is characterized by its liberal use of fresh herbs and spices, which add depth, complexity, and aroma to dishes. Ingredients such as ginger, garlic, lemongrass, and cilantro are commonly used to infuse dishes with bright, zesty flavors, while spices such as cinnamon, cloves, and star anise lend warmth and depth to curries, stews, and marinades.

Soy sauce, made from fermented soybeans and grains, is another indispensable ingredient in Asian cooking, prized for its rich umami flavor and savory depth. Used as a seasoning, marinade, or dipping sauce, soy sauce adds a distinctive salty-sweet flavor to dishes and helps to balance and enhance the other ingredients.

Similarly, ingredients such as miso paste, fermented tofu, and fish sauce are also commonly used to impart umami-rich flavors to dishes, while chili peppers, chili paste, and chili oil add fiery heat and spice. These ingredients are often used judiciously to create a harmonious balance of flavors, with each component working together to create a symphony of taste and texture.

When it comes to cooking techniques, Asian cuisine is known for its versatility and creativity, with dishes being prepared using a wide range of methods, from steaming and stir-frying to braising and deep-frying. Stir-frying, in particular, is a popular cooking technique in many Asian cuisines, where ingredients are quickly cooked over high heat in a wok, resulting in dishes that are tender, flavorful, and brightly colored.

Steaming is another common cooking technique in Asian cuisine, particularly in China, where it is used to prepare everything from dumplings and buns to whole fish and vegetables. Steaming is prized for its ability to preserve the natural flavors and nutrients of ingredients, resulting in dishes that are light, delicate, and healthful.

In addition to stir-frying and steaming, Asian cuisine also makes use of techniques such as braising, where ingredients are slowly simmered in flavorful liquid until tender, and deep-frying, where ingredients are submerged in hot oil until crisp and golden brown. These techniques allow chefs to create a wide variety of dishes with different textures, flavors, and appearances, making Asian cuisine as diverse and dynamic as the continent itself.

In conclusion, the ingredients and cooking techniques of Asian cuisine are as diverse and varied as the cultures and traditions that inspire them. From fragrant herbs and spices to hearty grains and noodles, Asian cuisine offers a rich tapestry of flavors, textures, and aromas that reflect the region's culinary heritage and ingenuity. By celebrating the abundance of nature and the artistry of cooking, Asian cuisine continues to inspire and delight diners around the world, inviting them on a journey of culinary discovery and exploration.

TIPS FOR SUCCESSFUL VEGAN ASIAN COOKING

Mastering vegan Asian cooking requires a combination of skill, knowledge, and creativity. To ensure successful outcomes, it's essential to understand the key principles and techniques that underpin this culinary tradition. Here are some tips to help you elevate your vegan Asian cooking:

1. Embrace Umami-rich Ingredients: Umami, often referred to as the fifth taste, is a savory flavor that adds depth and richness to dishes. Incorporate ingredients such as soy sauce, miso paste, mushrooms, and seaweed to enhance the umami profile of your vegan Asian dishes. These ingredients will impart a complex and satisfying flavor to your cooking.

2. Explore Plant-based Protein Sources: While meat and dairy products are commonly used in Asian cuisine, there are plenty of plant-based protein sources that can be used as substitutes. Tofu, tempeh, seitan, and legumes such as chickpeas and lentils are excellent alternatives that can be used to create hearty and satisfying vegan dishes. Experiment with different protein sources to discover new flavors and textures.

3. Balance Flavors and Textures: Asian cuisine is known for its balance of flavors and textures, with dishes often incorporating elements of sweet, sour, salty, and spicy. Pay attention to the interplay of these flavors and aim to achieve a harmonious balance in your dishes. Additionally, vary the textures of your ingredients by incorporating crunchy vegetables, tender proteins, and chewy noodles to create a more dynamic eating experience.

4. Harness the Power of Aromatics: Aromatics such as garlic, ginger, onions, and chilies are the foundation of many Asian dishes, imparting depth and complexity to the flavor profile. Learn to sauté, stir-fry, or simmer these ingredients to release their aromatic oils and enhance the overall flavor of your dishes. Experiment with different combinations of aromatics to create unique and memorable flavor profiles.

5. Utilize Traditional Cooking Techniques: Traditional Asian cooking techniques such as stir-frying, steaming, and braising are well-suited to vegan cooking and can help to preserve the natural flavors and textures of plant-based ingredients. Learn to master these techniques to achieve optimal results in your vegan Asian dishes. Additionally, don't be afraid to experiment with modern cooking methods such as pressure cooking or air frying to add variety to your repertoire.

6. Be Mindful of Seasonality: In Asian cuisine, seasonality plays a crucial role in ingredient selection and menu planning. Take advantage of seasonal produce to ensure that your dishes are fresh, flavorful, and environmentally sustainable. Incorporating seasonal fruits and vegetables will not only enhance the taste of your dishes but also connect you more deeply with the natural rhythms of the earth.

7. Experiment with Ethnic Varieties: Asian cuisine encompasses a diverse array of culinary traditions, each with its own unique flavors, ingredients, and cooking techniques. Take the time to explore the cuisines of different Asian countries, from the spicy curries of Thailand to the delicate sushi of Japan, and experiment with incorporating elements of these traditions into your vegan cooking. This will not only expand your culinary horizons but also inspire you to create new and exciting dishes.

8. Pay Attention to Presentation: In Asian cuisine, the presentation of a dish is just as important as its flavor. Take care to arrange your dishes thoughtfully, paying attention to color, texture, and composition. Garnish your dishes with fresh herbs, toasted nuts, or edible flowers to add visual interest and elevate the overall dining experience.

By following these tips, you can enhance your skills in vegan Asian cooking and create delicious, satisfying dishes that celebrate the flavors and traditions of the continent. Whether you're a seasoned chef or a novice cook, experimenting with vegan Asian cuisine is a rewarding and enjoyable experience that will expand your culinary repertoire and delight your taste buds.

APPETIZERS AND SMALL BITES

Fresh and Crispy Vegetable Spring Rolls

Prep: 20 mins | Cook: 10 mins | Serves: 4

Ingredients:

- 8 rice paper wrappers
- 2 cups shredded lettuce
- 1 cup shredded carrots
- 1 cucumber, julienned
- 1 bell pepper, thinly sliced
- 1 cup fresh mint leaves
- 1 cup fresh cilantro leaves
- Hoisin sauce, for dipping
- Sriracha, for dipping

Instructions:

1. **Prepare Ingredients:** Prepare all the vegetables and herbs as listed in the ingredients.
2. **Soak Rice Paper:** Fill a shallow dish with warm water. Dip one rice paper wrapper into the water for a few seconds until it softens.
3. **Assemble Spring Rolls:** Lay the softened rice paper on a clean surface. Place a small amount of lettuce, carrots, cucumber, bell pepper, mint leaves, and cilantro leaves in the center of the wrapper.
4. **Roll Spring Rolls:** Fold the bottom of the wrapper over the filling, then fold in the sides, and roll tightly to enclose the filling. Repeat with the remaining wrappers and filling.
5. **Serve:** Serve the spring rolls with hoisin sauce and sriracha for dipping.

Nutritional Info (per serving): Calories: 150 | Fat: 0.5g | Carbs: 35g | Protein: 3g

Edamame Dumplings with Soy-Ginger Dipping Sauce

Prep: 30 mins | Cook: 15 mins | Serves: 4

Ingredients:

- 1 cup shelled edamame
- 2 cloves garlic, minced
- 1 teaspoon grated ginger
- 2 green onions, finely chopped
- 1 tablespoon soy sauce

- 1 tablespoon sesame oil
- 24 round dumpling wrappers
- Sesame seeds, for garnish

Instructions:

1. Prepare Filling: In a food processor, pulse the edamame, garlic, ginger, green onions, soy sauce, and sesame oil until well combined but still slightly chunky.
2. Assemble Dumplings: Place a spoonful of the filling in the center of each dumpling wrapper. Moisten the edges with water, then fold the wrapper in half and pinch the edges to seal.
3. Steam Dumplings: Arrange the dumplings in a steamer basket lined with parchment paper. Steam for 10-12 minutes until cooked through.
4. Make Dipping Sauce: In a small bowl, mix together soy sauce and grated ginger to make the dipping sauce.
5. Serve: Sprinkle the steamed dumplings with sesame seeds and serve with the soy-ginger dipping sauce.

Nutritional Info (per serving): Calories: 180 | Fat: 3g | Carbs: 30g | Protein: 8g

Crispy Tofu Bites with Spicy Peanut Sauce

Prep: 15 mins | Cook: 20 mins | Serves: 4

Ingredients:

- 1 block firm tofu, pressed and cubed
- 1/4 cup cornstarch
- 1 teaspoon garlic powder
- 1 teaspoon smoked paprika
- Salt and pepper, to taste
- Cooking spray
- 1/4 cup peanut butter
- 2 tablespoons soy sauce
- 1 tablespoon rice vinegar
- 1 tablespoon maple syrup
- 1 clove garlic, minced
- 1 teaspoon grated ginger
- Sriracha, to taste
- Chopped peanuts, for garnish
- Sliced green onions, for garnish

Instructions:

1. Prepare Tofu: In a shallow dish, mix together cornstarch, garlic powder, smoked paprika, salt, and pepper. Dredge the tofu cubes in the cornstarch mixture until evenly coated.
2. Bake Tofu: Arrange the tofu cubes on a baking sheet lined with parchment paper. Lightly spray the tofu with cooking spray. Bake at 400°F (200°C) for 20-25 minutes until golden and crispy.
3. Make Peanut Sauce: In a small saucepan, combine peanut butter, soy sauce, rice vinegar, maple syrup, garlic, ginger, and sriracha. Cook over low heat, stirring constantly, until smooth and heated through.
4. Serve: Serve the crispy tofu bites with the spicy peanut sauce, garnished with chopped peanuts and sliced green onions.

Nutritional Info (per serving): Calories: 220 | Fat: 12g | Carbs: 15g | Protein: 15g

Refreshing Vietnamese Fresh Rolls with Peanut Dipping Sauce

Prep: 30 mins | Cook: 0 mins | Serves: 4

Ingredients:

- 8 rice paper wrappers
- 2 cups cooked rice vermicelli noodles
- 1 cup shredded lettuce
- 1 cup fresh mint leaves
- 1 cup fresh cilantro leaves
- 1 cucumber, julienned
- 1 carrot, julienned
- 1 bell pepper, thinly sliced
- 8 large cooked shrimp, halved lengthwise (optional)
- 1/4 cup peanuts, chopped (optional)
- Hoisin sauce, for dipping

Instructions:

1. Prepare Ingredients: Cook rice vermicelli noodles according to package instructions and prepare all vegetables and herbs as listed in the ingredients.
2. Soak Rice Paper: Fill a shallow dish with warm water. Dip one rice paper wrapper into the water for a few seconds until it softens.
3. Assemble Fresh Rolls: Lay the softened rice paper on a clean surface. Place a small amount of rice vermicelli noodles, lettuce, mint leaves, cilantro leaves, cucumber, carrot, bell pepper, and shrimp (if using) in the center of the wrapper.

4. **Roll Fresh Rolls:** Fold the bottom of the wrapper over the filling, then fold in the sides, and roll tightly to enclose the filling. Repeat with the remaining wrappers and filling.
5. **Serve:** Serve the fresh rolls with hoisin sauce for dipping. Garnish with chopped peanuts if desired.

Nutritional Info (per serving, without shrimp): Calories: 180 | Fat: 3g | Carbs: 35g | Protein: 5g

Tangy Mango Salad Rolls with Lime Dipping Sauce

Prep: 20 mins | Cook: 0 mins | Serves: 4

Ingredients:

- 8 rice paper wrappers
- 2 ripe mangoes, thinly sliced
- 2 cups cooked rice vermicelli noodles
- 1 cup shredded lettuce
- 1/2 cup fresh mint leaves
- 1/2 cup fresh cilantro leaves
- 1/4 cup chopped roasted peanuts
- Lime wedges, for serving
- Sweet chili sauce, for dipping

Instructions:

1. **Prepare Ingredients:** Cook rice vermicelli noodles according to package instructions and prepare all other ingredients as listed in the ingredients.
2. **Soak Rice Paper:** Fill a shallow dish with warm water. Dip one rice paper wrapper into the water for a few seconds until it softens.
3. **Assemble Salad Rolls:** Lay the softened rice paper on a clean surface. Place a few slices of mango, rice vermicelli noodles, lettuce, mint leaves, cilantro leaves, and chopped peanuts in the center of the wrapper.
4. **Roll Salad Rolls:** Fold the bottom of the wrapper over the filling, then fold in the sides, and roll tightly to enclose the filling. Repeat with the remaining wrappers and filling.
5. **Serve:** Serve the salad rolls with lime wedges and sweet chili sauce for dipping.

Nutritional Info (per serving): Calories: 220 | Fat: 5g | Carbs: 40g | Protein: 5g

Vegetable Samosas

Prep: 30 mins | Cook: 25 mins | Serves: 4

Ingredients:

- 2 cups all-purpose flour
- 1/4 cup vegetable oil
- 1 teaspoon cumin seeds
- 1 onion, finely chopped
- 2 potatoes, boiled and diced
- 1 cup mixed vegetables (peas, carrots, corn)
- 1 teaspoon garam masala
- 1 teaspoon turmeric
- Salt to taste
- Oil for frying

Instructions:

1. Make Dough: Mix flour, vegetable oil, and a pinch of salt in a bowl. Gradually add water to form a soft dough. Cover and let it rest for 30 minutes.
2. Prepare Filling: Heat oil in a pan. Add cumin seeds and onion. Sauté until onions are translucent. Add boiled potatoes, mixed vegetables, garam masala, turmeric, and salt. Cook for 5-7 minutes. Let the filling cool.
3. Shape Samosas: Divide the dough into small balls. Roll each ball into a circle and cut in half. Fold each half into a cone shape, fill with the vegetable mixture, and seal the edges.
4. Fry: Heat oil in a pan. Fry samosas until golden brown and crispy, about 3-4 minutes per side.
5. Serve: Drain on paper towels and serve hot with chutney or dipping sauce.

Nutritional Info: Calories: 320 | Fat: 15g | Carbs: 42g | Protein: 6g

Baked Veggie Pot Stickers

Prep: 30 mins | Cook: 25 mins | Serves: 4

Ingredients:

- 24 round pot sticker wrappers
- 2 cups mixed vegetables (cabbage, carrots, mushrooms), finely chopped
- 2 cloves garlic, minced
- 1 tablespoon soy sauce
- 1 teaspoon sesame oil

- 1 teaspoon grated ginger
- 2 green onions, chopped
- 2 tablespoons vegetable oil
- Sesame seeds for garnish

Instructions:

1. Prepare Filling: In a pan, sauté mixed vegetables, garlic, soy sauce, sesame oil, ginger, and green onions until tender. Let it cool.
2. Fill Wrappers: Place a spoonful of filling in the center of each pot sticker wrapper. Moisten the edges with water, then fold and pleat to seal.
3. Bake: Preheat oven to 375°F (190°C). Place pot stickers on a baking sheet lined with parchment paper. Lightly brush with vegetable oil and sprinkle sesame seeds on top. Bake for 20-25 minutes until golden brown and crispy.
4. Serve: Serve hot with soy sauce or dipping sauce of your choice.

Nutritional Info: Calories: 160 | Fat: 7g | Carbs: 20g | Protein: 5g

Avocado Cucumber Rolls

Prep: 15 mins | Cook: 0 mins | Serves: 2

Ingredients:

- 2 large cucumbers
- 1 ripe avocado, sliced
- 1/2 red bell pepper, julienned
- 1/4 cup shredded carrots
- 1/4 cup alfalfa sprouts
- 2 tablespoons sesame seeds
- Soy sauce for dipping

Instructions:

- Prepare Cucumbers: Peel cucumbers and slice lengthwise into thin strips using a vegetable peeler or mandoline slicer.
- Fill Cucumber Strips: Lay cucumber strips flat and place avocado slices, bell pepper, shredded carrots, and alfalfa sprouts on one end of each strip.
- Roll: Roll the cucumber strips tightly around the filling to form rolls.
- Slice and Serve: Use a sharp knife to slice rolls into bite-sized pieces. Arrange on a plate and sprinkle sesame seeds on top. Serve with soy sauce for dipping.

Nutritional Info: Calories: 180 | Fat: 10g | Carbs: 20g | Protein: 4g

Crispy Cauliflower Wings

Prep: 15 mins | Cook: 25 mins | Serves: 4

Ingredients:

- 1 head cauliflower, cut into florets
- 1 cup all-purpose flour
- 1 cup almond milk
- 1 teaspoon garlic powder
- 1 teaspoon paprika
- 1/2 teaspoon salt
- 1/4 teaspoon black pepper
- 1 cup breadcrumbs
- BBQ sauce for dipping

Instructions:

1. Preheat oven: Preheat oven to 425°F (220°C). Line a baking sheet with parchment paper.
2. Prepare Batter: In a bowl, whisk together flour, almond milk, garlic powder, paprika, salt, and black pepper until smooth.
3. Coat Cauliflower: Dip cauliflower florets into the batter, then roll in breadcrumbs until evenly coated.
4. Bake: Place coated cauliflower florets on the prepared baking sheet. Bake for 20-25 minutes, flipping halfway through, until crispy and golden brown.
5. Serve: Serve hot with BBQ sauce for dipping.

Nutritional Info: Calories: 220 | Fat: 5g | Carbs: 35g | Protein: 7g

Vegetable Tempura

Prep: 15 mins | Cook: 10 mins | Serves: 4

Ingredients:

- Assorted vegetables (such as sweet potatoes, bell peppers, broccoli, and mushrooms), sliced
- 1 cup all-purpose flour
- 1 cup ice-cold water
- 1/4 teaspoon baking powder
- Oil for frying
- Dipping sauce (soy sauce, rice vinegar, and grated ginger) for serving

Instructions:

1. Prepare Vegetables: Slice assorted vegetables into thin pieces.
2. Make Batter: In a bowl, whisk together flour, ice-cold water, and baking powder until just combined. Do not overmix; lumps are okay.
3. Heat Oil: Heat oil in a deep fryer or large pot to 350°F (180°C).
4. Coat Vegetables: Dip vegetable slices into the batter, ensuring they are fully coated.
5. Fry: Carefully place battered vegetables into the hot oil, frying in batches to avoid overcrowding the pot. Fry until golden brown and crispy, about 2-3 minutes per batch.
6. Drain and Serve: Remove fried vegetables from the oil and place on a plate lined with paper towels to drain excess oil. Serve hot with dipping sauce.

Nutritional Info: Calories: 150 | Fat: 3g | Carbs: 30g | Protein: 4g

Sweet Chili Tofu Bites

Prep: 20 mins | Cook: 20 mins | Serves: 4

Ingredients:

- 1 block firm tofu, pressed and cubed
- 1/4 cup cornstarch
- Oil for frying
- Sweet chili sauce for dipping

Instructions:

1. Coat Tofu: Toss tofu cubes in cornstarch until evenly coated.
2. Fry: Heat oil in a pan. Fry tofu cubes until golden brown and crispy, about 4-5 minutes per side.
3. Serve: Serve hot with sweet chili sauce for dipping.

Nutritional Info: Calories: 200 | Fat: 8g | Carbs: 25g | Protein: 10g

Vegan Shumai Dumplings

Prep: 30 mins | Cook: 15 mins | Serves: 4

Ingredients:

- 24 round dumpling wrappers
- 1 cup finely chopped mushrooms (shiitake or button)
- 1 cup finely chopped cabbage
- 1/4 cup finely chopped carrots
- 2 cloves garlic, minced
- 1 tablespoon soy sauce

- 1 tablespoon sesame oil
- 1 teaspoon grated ginger
- 2 green onions, chopped
- Sesame seeds for garnish

Instructions:

1. Prepare Filling: In a pan, sauté mushrooms, cabbage, carrots, garlic, soy sauce, sesame oil, ginger, and green onions until vegetables are tender. Let the filling cool.
2. Fill Wrappers: Place a spoonful of filling in the center of each dumpling wrapper. Moisten the edges with water, then fold and pleat to seal.
3. Steam: Arrange dumplings in a steamer basket lined with parchment paper. Steam for 10-12 minutes until dumplings are cooked through.
4. Serve: Sprinkle sesame seeds on top and serve hot with soy sauce or dipping sauce of your choice.

Nutritional Info: Calories: 160 | Fat: 5g | Carbs: 25g | Protein: 5g

Baked Veggie Samosa Bites

Prep: 30 mins | Cook: 25 mins | Serves: 4

Ingredients:

- 10 sheets phyllo pastry
- 2 cups boiled and mashed potatoes
- 1/2 cup green peas
- 1/4 cup chopped cilantro
- 1 teaspoon cumin seeds
- 1 teaspoon garam masala
- 1 teaspoon turmeric
- Salt to taste
- Oil for brushing

Instructions:

1. Prepare Filling: In a bowl, mix mashed potatoes, green peas, cilantro, cumin seeds, garam masala, turmeric, and salt until well combined.
2. Assemble Samosa Bites: Cut each phyllo sheet into 3 strips. Place a spoonful of filling at one end of each strip, then fold diagonally to form a triangle. Continue folding until the entire strip is used. Repeat with remaining ingredients.
3. Bake: Preheat oven to 375°F (190°C). Place samosa bites on a baking sheet lined with parchment paper. Brush with oil. Bake for 20-25 minutes until golden brown and crispy.

4. Serve: Serve hot with chutney or dipping sauce.

Nutritional Info: Calories: 180 | Fat: 4g | Carbs: 30g | Protein: 5g

Vegan Scallion Pancakes

Prep: 15 mins | Cook: 15 mins | Serves: 2

Ingredients:

- 2 cups all-purpose flour
- 1 cup warm water
- 1/4 cup chopped scallions
- 2 tablespoons vegetable oil
- Salt to taste
- Soy sauce for dipping

Instructions:

1. Make Dough: In a bowl, mix flour, warm water, and salt until a smooth dough forms. Let it rest for 10 minutes.
2. Roll Out Dough: Divide dough into 4 equal portions. Roll each portion into a thin circle.
3. Add Scallions: Brush each circle with vegetable oil and sprinkle chopped scallions evenly over the surface.
4. Roll and Flatten: Roll up each circle into a tight cylinder, then coil it into a round pancake. Flatten the pancake with your palm.
5. Pan-Fry: Heat oil in a non-stick pan over medium heat. Cook pancakes for 3-4 minutes on each side until golden brown and crispy.
6. Serve: Cut pancakes into wedges and serve hot with soy sauce for dipping.

Nutritional Info: Calories: 250 | Fat: 7g | Carbs: 40g | Protein: 6g

Crispy Vegetable Fritters

Prep: 20 mins | Cook: 15 mins | Serves: 4

Ingredients:

- 1 cup chickpea flour
- 1/2 cup water
- 1/2 teaspoon baking powder
- 1/2 teaspoon turmeric
- 1/2 teaspoon cumin
- 1/2 teaspoon paprika
- 1 cup shredded zucchini

- 1 cup shredded carrots
- 1/2 cup chopped spinach
- Salt and pepper to taste
- Oil for frying

Instructions:

1. Make Batter: In a bowl, mix chickpea flour, water, baking powder, turmeric, cumin, and paprika until smooth.
2. Add Vegetables: Stir in shredded zucchini, carrots, chopped spinach, salt, and pepper until well combined.
3. Fry: Heat oil in a pan over medium heat. Drop spoonfuls of batter into the hot oil and flatten slightly with the back of a spoon. Fry until golden brown and crispy, about 3-4 minutes per side.
4. Serve: Drain on paper towels and serve hot with your favorite dipping sauce.

Nutritional Info: Calories: 220 | Fat: 8g | Carbs: 30g | Protein: 8g

SOUPS AND BROTHS

Vegan Hot and Sour Soup

Prep: 15 mins | Cook: 20 mins | Serves: 4

Ingredients:

- 4 cups vegetable broth
- 1/4 cup rice vinegar
- 2 tablespoons soy sauce
- 1 tablespoon chili paste
- 1 tablespoon sesame oil
- 1 tablespoon cornstarch
- 1 cup sliced mushrooms
- 1/2 cup bamboo shoots, sliced
- 1/2 cup tofu, diced
- 1/4 cup sliced green onions
- 1/4 cup sliced tofu skin (optional)
- Salt and pepper to taste

Instructions:

1. Prepare Broth: In a pot, combine vegetable broth, rice vinegar, soy sauce, chili paste, and sesame oil. Bring to a simmer.
2. Thicken Soup: In a small bowl, mix cornstarch with a bit of water to create a slurry. Stir into the simmering broth to thicken.
3. Add Ingredients: Add mushrooms, bamboo shoots, tofu, green onions, and tofu skin (if using) to the pot. Simmer for 10-15 minutes until mushrooms are tender and flavors meld.
4. Season: Season with salt and pepper to taste.
5. Serve: Ladle hot soup into bowls and serve immediately.

Nutritional Info: Calories: 120 | Fat: 6g | Carbs: 10g | Protein: 8g

Miso Soup

Prep: 10 mins | Cook: 10 mins | Serves: 4

Ingredients:

- 4 cups vegetable broth
- 1/4 cup miso paste
- 1 cup cubed tofu
- 1/2 cup sliced green onions
- 1/2 cup sliced mushrooms
- 2 sheets nori, torn into small pieces
- 1 tablespoon soy sauce
- 1 tablespoon sesame oil
- Salt and pepper to taste

Instructions:

1. Heat Broth: In a pot, heat vegetable broth until simmering.
2. Dissolve Miso: In a small bowl, whisk miso paste with a bit of hot broth until smooth. Stir into the pot.
3. Add Ingredients: Add tofu, green onions, mushrooms, nori, soy sauce, and sesame oil to the pot. Simmer for 5-7 minutes until heated through.
4. Season: Season with salt and pepper to taste.
5. Serve: Ladle hot soup into bowls and serve immediately.

Nutritional Info: Calories: 140 | Fat: 7g | Carbs: 9g | Protein: 10g

Vegetable Wonton Soup

Prep: 30 mins | Cook: 15 mins | Serves: 4

Ingredients:

- 24 vegan wonton wrappers
- 2 cups vegetable broth
- 1 cup water
- 1 cup sliced mushrooms
- 1/2 cup shredded cabbage
- 1/4 cup shredded carrots
- 1/4 cup sliced green onions
- 1 tablespoon soy sauce
- 1 tablespoon sesame oil
- Salt and pepper to taste

Instructions:

1. Prepare Broth: In a pot, combine vegetable broth and water. Bring to a simmer.
2. Add Vegetables: Add mushrooms, cabbage, carrots, and green onions to the pot. Simmer for 5-7 minutes until vegetables are tender.
3. Season: Stir in soy sauce and sesame oil. Season with salt and pepper to taste.
4. Cook Wontons: Bring a separate pot of water to a boil. Drop wonton wrappers into the boiling water and cook for 3-4 minutes until they float to the surface.
5. Assemble Soup: Divide cooked wontons among serving bowls. Ladle hot broth and vegetables over the wontons.
6. Serve: Garnish with additional green onions if desired and serve hot.

Nutritional Info: Calories: 180 | Fat: 5g | Carbs: 25g | Protein: 8g

Thai Coconut Soup

Prep: 15 mins | Cook: 20 mins | Serves: 4

Ingredients:

- 4 cups vegetable broth
- 1 can (14 oz) coconut milk
- 2 tablespoons red curry paste
- 1 tablespoon soy sauce
- 1 tablespoon brown sugar
- 1 cup sliced mushrooms
- 1/2 cup sliced bell peppers
- 1/2 cup sliced bamboo shoots
- 1/4 cup chopped cilantro
- Juice of 1 lime
- Salt and pepper to taste

Instructions:

1. Simmer Soup: In a pot, combine vegetable broth, coconut milk, red curry paste, soy sauce, and brown sugar. Bring to a simmer.
2. Add Vegetables: Add mushrooms, bell peppers, and bamboo shoots to the pot. Simmer for 10-15 minutes until vegetables are tender.
3. Finish Soup: Stir in chopped cilantro and lime juice. Season with salt and pepper to taste.
4. Serve: Ladle hot soup into bowls and serve immediately.

Nutritional Info: Calories: 250 | Fat: 20g | Carbs: 15g | Protein: 5g

Vietnamese Pho

Prep: 30 mins | Cook: 2 hours | Serves: 4

Ingredients:

- 8 cups vegetable broth
- 2 cinnamon sticks
- 4 star anise
- 1 tablespoon whole cloves
- 1 tablespoon coriander seeds
- 1 tablespoon grated ginger
- 1 tablespoon soy sauce
- 1 tablespoon maple syrup
- 1 package (14 oz) rice noodles
- 1 cup sliced mushrooms
- 1 cup bean sprouts
- 1/2 cup sliced green onions
- Fresh cilantro, Thai basil, and lime wedges for serving

Instructions:

1. Infuse Broth: In a large pot, combine vegetable broth, cinnamon sticks, star anise, cloves, coriander seeds, grated ginger, soy sauce, and maple syrup. Simmer for 1-2 hours to infuse flavors.
2. Cook Noodles: Cook rice noodles according to package instructions. Drain and set aside.
3. Prepare Toppings: Arrange sliced mushrooms, bean sprouts, sliced green onions, cilantro, Thai basil, and lime wedges on a serving platter.
4. Assemble Pho: Divide cooked noodles among serving bowls. Ladle hot broth over the noodles, straining out the whole spices.
5. Serve: Serve hot with prepared toppings. Let diners customize their pho with herbs, lime juice, and sauces as desired.

Nutritional Info: Calories: 300 | Fat: 2g | Carbs: 60g | Protein: 8g

Vegetable Laksa

Prep: 20 mins | Cook: 25 mins | Serves: 4

Ingredients:

- 2 tablespoons vegetable oil
- 1 onion, chopped
- 2 cloves garlic, minced
- 2 tablespoons laksa paste
- 4 cups vegetable broth
- 1 can (14 oz) coconut milk
- 1 tablespoon soy sauce
- 1 tablespoon brown sugar
- 1 cup sliced mushrooms
- 1 cup sliced bell peppers
- 1 cup sliced tofu
- 1 cup bean sprouts
- 8 oz rice noodles
- Fresh cilantro and lime wedges for serving

Instructions:

1. Sauté Aromatics: Heat vegetable oil in a pot over medium heat. Add chopped onion and minced garlic. Sauté until softened, about 2-3 minutes.
2. Add Laksa Paste: Stir in laksa paste and cook for another 2 minutes until fragrant.
3. Simmer Soup: Pour in vegetable broth and coconut milk. Add soy sauce and brown sugar. Bring to a simmer.
4. Cook Vegetables and Tofu: Add sliced mushrooms, bell peppers, tofu, and bean sprouts to the pot. Simmer for 10-15 minutes until vegetables are tender.
5. Cook Noodles: Meanwhile, cook rice noodles according to package instructions. Drain and set aside.
6. Assemble Laksa: Divide cooked noodles among serving bowls. Ladle hot laksa soup over the noodles and vegetables.
7. Serve: Garnish with fresh cilantro and lime wedges. Serve hot.

Nutritional Info: Calories: 380 | Fat: 20g | Carbs: 40g | Protein: 10g

Vegan Ramen

Prep: 15 mins | Cook: 25 mins | Serves: 4

Ingredients:

- 8 cups vegetable broth
- 4 cloves garlic, minced
- 2 tablespoons grated ginger
- 1 tablespoon miso paste
- 2 tablespoons soy sauce
- 1 tablespoon sesame oil
- 8 oz ramen noodles
- 1 cup sliced mushrooms
- 1 cup shredded cabbage
- 1 cup sliced carrots
- 1 cup baby spinach
- 4 sheets nori, torn into small pieces
- Sliced green onions and sesame seeds for serving

Instructions:

1. Prepare Broth: In a pot, combine vegetable broth, minced garlic, grated ginger, miso paste, soy sauce, and sesame oil. Bring to a simmer.
2. Cook Ramen Noodles: Add ramen noodles to the simmering broth. Cook according to package instructions until noodles are tender.
3. Add Vegetables: Stir in sliced mushrooms, shredded cabbage, sliced carrots, and baby spinach. Simmer for 5-7 minutes until vegetables are tender.
4. Serve: Ladle hot ramen soup into bowls. Top with torn nori, sliced green onions, and sesame seeds. Serve hot.

Nutritional Info: Calories: 320 | Fat: 8g | Carbs: 50g | Protein: 12g

Spicy Kimchi Soup

Prep: 15 mins | Cook: 20 mins | Serves: 4

Ingredients:

- 4 cups vegetable broth
- 1 cup vegan kimchi
- 1 tablespoon gochujang (Korean chili paste)
- 1 tablespoon soy sauce
- 1 tablespoon sesame oil

- 1 cup sliced mushrooms
- 1 cup diced tofu
- 1 cup sliced green onions
- 1 cup sliced cabbage
- Cooked rice for serving
- Fresh cilantro and sesame seeds for garnish

Instructions:

1. Simmer Soup: In a pot, combine vegetable broth, vegan kimchi, gochujang, soy sauce, and sesame oil. Bring to a simmer.
2. Add Ingredients: Stir in sliced mushrooms, diced tofu, sliced green onions, and sliced cabbage. Simmer for 10-15 minutes until vegetables are tender.
3. Serve: Ladle hot soup into bowls. Serve with cooked rice on the side. Garnish with fresh cilantro and sesame seeds.

Nutritional Info: Calories: 280 | Fat: 10g | Carbs: 25g | Protein: 15g

Vegan Congee

Prep: 10 mins | Cook: 1 hour | Serves: 4

Ingredients:

- 1 cup jasmine rice
- 8 cups vegetable broth
- 1 tablespoon grated ginger
- 1 tablespoon soy sauce
- 1 tablespoon sesame oil
- Toppings: sliced green onions, fried tofu, sliced mushrooms, crispy shallots

Instructions:

1. Cook Congee: Rinse jasmine rice under cold water until the water runs clear. In a large pot, combine rice, vegetable broth, grated ginger, soy sauce, and sesame oil. Bring to a boil, then reduce heat to low and simmer for 1 hour, stirring occasionally, until the rice is soft and creamy.
2. Serve: Ladle hot congee into bowls. Top with sliced green onions, fried tofu, sliced mushrooms, and crispy shallots.

Nutritional Info: Calories: 220 | Fat: 6g | Carbs: 35g | Protein: 8g

Vegetable Dumpling Soup

Prep: 30 mins | Cook: 20 mins | Serves: 4

Ingredients:

- 24 vegan dumplings
- 6 cups vegetable broth
- 1 cup sliced mushrooms
- 1 cup shredded cabbage
- 1/2 cup shredded carrots
- 1/4 cup sliced green onions
- 1 tablespoon soy sauce
- 1 tablespoon sesame oil
- Salt and pepper to taste

Instructions:

1. Simmer Soup: In a pot, bring vegetable broth to a simmer.
2. Add Dumplings: Add vegan dumplings to the simmering broth. Cook according to package instructions until dumplings are cooked through.
3. Add Vegetables: Stir in sliced mushrooms, shredded cabbage, shredded carrots, and sliced green onions. Simmer for 5-7 minutes until vegetables are tender.
4. Season: Stir in soy sauce and sesame oil. Season with salt and pepper to taste.
5. Serve: Ladle hot soup into bowls and serve immediately.

Nutritional Info: Calories: 280 | Fat: 10g | Carbs: 35g | Protein: 12g

Mushroom Miso Soup

Prep: 15 mins | Cook: 20 mins | Serves: 4

Ingredients:

- 4 cups vegetable broth
- 1/4 cup miso paste
- 1 cup sliced mushrooms
- 1/2 cup sliced green onions
- 1/2 cup diced tofu
- 1 tablespoon soy sauce
- 1 tablespoon sesame oil
- 1 tablespoon rice vinegar
- 1 teaspoon grated ginger
- 1 clove garlic, minced

- Salt and pepper to taste
- Toasted sesame seeds for garnish

Instructions:

1. Prepare Broth: In a pot, bring vegetable broth to a gentle simmer.
2. Dissolve Miso: In a small bowl, dissolve miso paste in a ladleful of hot broth. Stir until smooth, then add back to the pot.
3. Add Ingredients: Add sliced mushrooms, green onions, diced tofu, soy sauce, sesame oil, rice vinegar, grated ginger, and minced garlic to the pot. Simmer for 10-15 minutes until mushrooms are tender and flavors meld.
4. Season: Season with salt and pepper to taste.
5. Serve: Ladle hot soup into bowls, garnish with toasted sesame seeds, and serve immediately.

Nutritional Info: Calories: 150 | Fat: 8g | Carbs: 12g | Protein: 9g

Vegetable Tom Kha Soup

Prep: 20 mins | Cook: 20 mins | Serves: 4

Ingredients:

- 4 cups vegetable broth
- 1 can (14 oz) coconut milk
- 2 stalks lemongrass, bruised and chopped
- 4 kaffir lime leaves
- 1 tablespoon grated ginger
- 2 cloves garlic, minced
- 1 cup sliced mushrooms
- 1 cup sliced bell peppers
- 1 cup diced tofu
- 1 tablespoon soy sauce
- 1 tablespoon lime juice
- 1 tablespoon brown sugar
- Salt and pepper to taste
- Fresh cilantro for garnish

Instructions:

1. Simmer Aromatics: In a pot, combine vegetable broth, coconut milk, lemongrass, kaffir lime leaves, grated ginger, and minced garlic. Bring to a simmer and cook for 10 minutes to infuse flavors.

2. **Add Vegetables and Tofu:** Add sliced mushrooms, bell peppers, diced tofu, soy sauce, lime juice, and brown sugar to the pot. Simmer for another 10 minutes until vegetables are tender.
3. **Season:** Season with salt and pepper to taste.
4. **Serve:** Ladle hot soup into bowls, garnish with fresh cilantro, and serve immediately.

Nutritional Info: Calories: 200 | Fat: 12g | Carbs: 15g | Protein: 8g

Vegan Mulligatawny Soup

Prep: 20 mins | Cook: 30 mins | Serves: 4

Ingredients:

- 2 tablespoons vegetable oil
- 1 onion, chopped
- 2 carrots, diced
- 2 celery stalks, diced
- 2 cloves garlic, minced
- 1 tablespoon curry powder
- 1 teaspoon ground cumin
- 1/2 teaspoon ground coriander
- 1/4 teaspoon cayenne pepper
- 4 cups vegetable broth
- 1 can (14 oz) diced tomatoes
- 1 cup red lentils, rinsed
- 1 cup diced potatoes
- 1 cup diced apples
- 1/2 cup coconut milk
- Salt and pepper to taste
- Fresh cilantro for garnish

Instructions:

1. **Sauté Aromatics:** In a pot, heat vegetable oil over medium heat. Add chopped onion, diced carrots, and diced celery. Sauté until softened, about 5 minutes.
2. **Add Spices:** Stir in minced garlic, curry powder, ground cumin, ground coriander, and cayenne pepper. Cook for another 2 minutes until fragrant.
3. **Simmer Soup:** Pour in vegetable broth, diced tomatoes, red lentils, diced potatoes, and diced apples. Bring to a boil, then reduce heat and simmer for 20-25 minutes until lentils and vegetables are tender.
4. **Add Coconut Milk:** Stir in coconut milk and simmer for another 5 minutes.

5. Season: Season with salt and pepper to taste.
6. Serve: Ladle hot soup into bowls, garnish with fresh cilantro, and serve immediately.

Nutritional Info: Calories: 280 | Fat: 10g | Carbs: 40g | Protein: 10g

Vegan Pho Broth

Prep: 15 mins | Cook: 1 hour | Serves: 4

Ingredients:

- 8 cups vegetable broth
- 1 onion, halved
- 3-inch piece of ginger, sliced
- 4 star anise
- 4 cloves
- 1 cinnamon stick
- 1 teaspoon coriander seeds
- 1 tablespoon soy sauce
- 1 tablespoon maple syrup
- Salt and pepper to taste

Instructions:

1. Char Aromatics: Preheat broiler. Place halved onion and sliced ginger on a baking sheet. Broil for 5-7 minutes until charred.
2. Simmer Broth: In a large pot, combine vegetable broth, charred onion, charred ginger, star anise, cloves, cinnamon stick, coriander seeds, soy sauce, and maple syrup. Bring to a boil, then reduce heat and simmer for 1 hour.
3. Strain: Strain the broth through a fine-mesh sieve, discarding solids.
4. Season: Season with salt and pepper to taste.
5. Serve: Use the pho broth as a base for assembling vegan pho bowls with noodles, tofu, vegetables, and herbs.

Nutritional Info: Calories: 50 | Fat: 0g | Carbs: 10g | Protein: 2g

Vegetable Soybean Soup

Prep: 20 mins | Cook: 30 mins | Serves: 4

Ingredients:

- 1 cup dried soybeans, soaked overnight
- 8 cups vegetable broth
- 1 onion, chopped
- 2 carrots, diced
- 2 celery stalks, diced
- 2 cloves garlic, minced
- 1 tablespoon soy sauce
- 1 tablespoon miso paste
- 1 tablespoon sesame oil
- Salt and pepper to taste
- Sliced green onions for garnish

Instructions:

1. Cook Soybeans: Drain soaked soybeans and rinse under cold water. In a pot, combine soybeans and vegetable broth. Bring to a boil, then reduce heat and simmer for 1 hour or until soybeans are tender.
2. Sauté Aromatics: In another pot, heat sesame oil over medium heat. Add chopped onion, diced carrots, diced celery, and minced garlic. Sauté until vegetables are tender, about 5-7 minutes.
3. Combine Ingredients: Add cooked soybeans and broth to the pot with sautéed vegetables. Stir in soy sauce and miso paste. Simmer for another 15-20 minutes to allow flavors to meld.
4. Season: Season with salt and pepper to taste.
5. Serve: Ladle hot soup into bowls, garnish with sliced green onions, and serve immediately.

Nutritional Info: Calories: 250 | Fat: 8g | Carbs: 30g | Protein: 15g

SALADS AND SIDE DISHES

Vegan Sushi Salad

Prep: 20 mins | Cook: 20 mins | Serves: 4

Ingredients:

- 2 cups sushi rice
- 3 tablespoons rice vinegar
- 2 tablespoons sugar
- 1 teaspoon salt
- 1 cucumber, julienned
- 1 carrot, julienned
- 1 avocado, sliced
- 1/2 cup edamame, shelled
- 4 nori sheets, torn into small pieces
- Soy sauce and wasabi for serving

Instructions:

1. Cook Sushi Rice: Rinse sushi rice under cold water until the water runs clear. Cook rice according to package instructions. Let it cool slightly.
2. Prepare Seasoning: In a small saucepan, heat rice vinegar, sugar, and salt until sugar and salt dissolve. Pour over cooked rice and gently fold to combine.
3. Assemble Salad: Divide seasoned sushi rice among serving bowls. Arrange julienned cucumber, carrot, avocado slices, edamame, and torn nori sheets on top of the rice.
4. Serve: Serve with soy sauce and wasabi on the side. Enjoy your deconstructed sushi bowl!

Nutritional Info: Calories: 300 | Fat: 7g | Carbs: 55g | Protein: 6g

Thai Mango Salad

Prep: 15 mins | Cook: 0 mins | Serves: 4

Ingredients:

- 2 ripe mangoes, peeled and sliced
- 1 red bell pepper, julienned
- 1/2 cup shredded carrots
- 1/4 cup chopped fresh cilantro
- 1/4 cup chopped fresh mint

- 1/4 cup chopped peanuts
- 1/4 cup lime juice
- 2 tablespoons soy sauce
- 1 tablespoon maple syrup
- 1 tablespoon sesame oil
- 1 teaspoon grated ginger
- 1 clove garlic, minced
- Red chili flakes (optional)

Instructions:

1. Prepare Dressing: In a small bowl, whisk together lime juice, soy sauce, maple syrup, sesame oil, grated ginger, minced garlic, and red chili flakes if using. Set aside.
2. Assemble Salad: In a large bowl, combine sliced mangoes, julienned red bell pepper, shredded carrots, chopped cilantro, and chopped mint.
3. Add Dressing: Pour the prepared dressing over the salad ingredients. Toss gently to coat everything evenly.
4. Serve: Garnish with chopped peanuts and serve immediately as a refreshing side dish or light lunch.

Nutritional Info: Calories: 200 | Fat: 8g | Carbs: 30g | Protein: 4g

Chinese Cucumber Salad

Prep: 10 mins | Cook: 0 mins | Serves: 4

Ingredients:

- 2 English cucumbers, thinly sliced
- 2 tablespoons rice vinegar
- 1 tablespoon soy sauce
- 1 tablespoon sesame oil
- 1 teaspoon sugar
- 1/2 teaspoon grated ginger
- 1 clove garlic, minced
- 1 tablespoon toasted sesame seeds
- Chopped green onions for garnish

Instructions:

1. Prepare Dressing: In a small bowl, whisk together rice vinegar, soy sauce, sesame oil, sugar, grated ginger, and minced garlic until well combined.
2. Marinate Cucumbers: Place thinly sliced cucumbers in a large bowl. Pour the dressing over the cucumbers and toss to coat evenly.
3. Chill: Cover the bowl and refrigerate for at least 30 minutes to allow the flavors to meld.
4. Serve: Sprinkle with toasted sesame seeds and chopped green onions before serving. Enjoy the refreshing crunch of this Chinese cucumber salad!

Nutritional Info: Calories: 50 | Fat: 3g | Carbs: 6g | Protein: 2g

Korean Bulgogi Lettuce Wraps

Prep: 15 mins | Cook: 10 mins | Serves: 4

Ingredients:

- 1 block extra-firm tofu, pressed and cubed
- 1/2 cup bulgogi marinade (store-bought or homemade)
- 1 tablespoon vegetable oil
- 1 head butter lettuce, leaves separated
- 1/4 cup sliced green onions
- 1/4 cup shredded carrots
- 1/4 cup shredded red cabbage
- Toasted sesame seeds for garnish

Instructions:

1. Marinate Tofu: In a bowl, toss cubed tofu with bulgogi marinade until well coated. Let it marinate for at least 15 minutes.
2. Cook Tofu: Heat vegetable oil in a skillet over medium heat. Add marinated tofu and cook for 5-7 minutes until browned and crispy.
3. Assemble Lettuce Wraps: Place a spoonful of cooked tofu on each lettuce leaf. Top with sliced green onions, shredded carrots, and shredded red cabbage.
4. Serve: Garnish with toasted sesame seeds and serve immediately. Enjoy these flavorful Korean lettuce wraps as a light and delicious appetizer or main dish!

Nutritional Info: Calories: 150 | Fat:5g | Carbs: 10g | Protein: 8g

Vietnamese Noodle Salad

Prep: 20 mins | Cook: 10 mins | Serves: 4

Ingredients:

- 8 oz rice vermicelli noodles
- 1 cup shredded lettuce
- 1 cup bean sprouts
- 1 cucumber, julienned
- 1 carrot, julienned
- 1/4 cup chopped fresh mint
- 1/4 cup chopped fresh cilantro
- 1/4 cup chopped peanuts
- Lime wedges for serving

For the Dressing:

- 1/4 cup soy sauce
- 2 tablespoons lime juice
- 2 tablespoons rice vinegar
- 2 tablespoons maple syrup
- 1 tablespoon sesame oil
- 1 clove garlic, minced
- 1 teaspoon grated ginger
- Red chili flakes to taste (optional)

Instructions:

1. Cook Noodles: Cook rice vermicelli noodles according to package instructions. Drain and rinse under cold water. Set aside.
2. Prepare Dressing: In a small bowl, whisk together soy sauce, lime juice, rice vinegar, maple syrup, sesame oil, minced garlic, grated ginger, and red chili flakes if using.
3. Assemble Salad: In a large bowl, combine cooked noodles, shredded lettuce, bean sprouts, julienned cucumber, julienned carrot, chopped mint, and chopped cilantro.
4. Add Dressing: Pour the prepared dressing over the salad ingredients. Toss gently to coat everything evenly.
5. Serve: Garnish with chopped peanuts and lime wedges. Serve immediately as a refreshing and satisfying meal.

Nutritional Info: Calories: 300 | Fat: 7g | Carbs: 55g | Protein: 8g

Japanese Potato Salad

Prep: 20 mins | Cook: 15 mins | Serves: 4

Ingredients:

- 4 medium potatoes, peeled and cubed
- 1 carrot, peeled and diced
- 1/2 cup frozen peas, thawed
- 1/4 cup vegan mayonnaise
- 2 tablespoons rice vinegar
- 1 tablespoon sugar
- 1 teaspoon salt
- 1/4 teaspoon black pepper
- Chopped fresh chives for garnish

Instructions:

1. Boil Potatoes: In a pot of salted water, boil cubed potatoes and diced carrot until fork-tender, about 10-12 minutes. Drain and let cool slightly.
2. Mash Potatoes: Transfer boiled potatoes and carrots to a large bowl. Add thawed peas, vegan mayonnaise, rice vinegar, sugar, salt, and black pepper. Mash until desired consistency is reached.
3. Chill: Cover the bowl and refrigerate for at least 1 hour to chill and allow the flavors to meld.
4. Serve: Garnish with chopped fresh chives before serving. Enjoy this creamy Japanese potato salad as a delightful side dish!

Nutritional Info: Calories: 200 | Fat: 5g | Carbs: 35g | Protein: 5g

Vegan Egg Roll in a Bowl

Prep: 15 mins | Cook: 15 mins | Serves: 4

Ingredients:

- 1 tablespoon sesame oil
- 1 onion, diced
- 2 cloves garlic, minced
- 1 tablespoon grated ginger
- 1/2 head cabbage, shredded
- 2 carrots, julienned
- 1 bell pepper, sliced
- 1/4 cup soy sauce

- 1 tablespoon rice vinegar
- 1 tablespoon maple syrup
- 1 teaspoon sriracha (optional)
- Sliced green onions for garnish
- Toasted sesame seeds for garnish

Instructions:

1. Sauté Aromatics: Heat sesame oil in a large skillet or wok over medium heat. Add diced onion, minced garlic, and grated ginger. Sauté until fragrant, about 2 minutes.
2. Add Vegetables: Add shredded cabbage, julienned carrots, and sliced bell pepper to the skillet. Cook, stirring occasionally, until vegetables are tender yet still crisp, about 5-7 minutes.
3. Prepare Sauce: In a small bowl, whisk together soy sauce, rice vinegar, maple syrup, and sriracha if using. Pour the sauce over the cooked vegetables in the skillet.
4. Toss: Toss everything together until the vegetables are evenly coated with the sauce. Cook for an additional 2-3 minutes to heat through.
5. Serve: Garnish with sliced green onions and toasted sesame seeds before serving. Enjoy this deconstructed egg roll in a bowl as a quick and flavorful meal!

Nutritional Info: Calories: 150 | Fat: 4g | Carbs: 25g | Protein: 5g

Spicy Cucumber Salad

Prep: 10 mins | Cook: 0 mins | Serves: 4

Ingredients:

- 2 English cucumbers, thinly sliced
- 1/4 cup rice vinegar
- 1 tablespoon soy sauce
- 1 tablespoon maple syrup
- 1 teaspoon sesame oil
- 1 clove garlic, minced
- 1 teaspoon grated ginger
- Red pepper flakes to taste
- Toasted sesame seeds for garnish

Instructions:

1. Prepare Dressing: In a small bowl, whisk together rice vinegar, soy sauce, maple syrup, sesame oil, minced garlic, grated ginger, and red pepper flakes to taste.
2. Marinate Cucumbers: Place thinly sliced cucumbers in a large bowl. Pour the dressing over the cucumbers and toss to coat evenly.
3. Chill: Cover the bowl and refrigerate for at least 30 minutes to allow the flavors to meld and the cucumbers to marinate.
4. Serve: Garnish with toasted sesame seeds before serving. Enjoy this tangy and spicy cucumber salad as a refreshing side dish or appetizer!

Nutritional Info: Calories: 40 | Fat: 1g | Carbs: 8g | Protein: 1g

Vegetable Pad Thai Salad

Prep: 20 mins | Cook: 10 mins | Serves: 4

Ingredients:

- 8 oz rice noodles
- 1 tablespoon vegetable oil
- 1 onion, thinly sliced
- 2 cloves garlic, minced
- 1 carrot, julienned
- 1 bell pepper, thinly sliced
- 1 cup bean sprouts
- 2 green onions, sliced
- 1/4 cup chopped peanuts
- Lime wedges for serving
- Chopped fresh cilantro for garnish

For the Sauce:

- 1/4 cup soy sauce
- 2 tablespoons lime juice
- 2 tablespoons maple syrup
- 1 tablespoon rice vinegar
- 1 tablespoon tamarind paste
- 1 teaspoon sriracha (optional)

Instructions:

1. **Cook Rice Noodles:** Cook rice noodles according to package instructions. Drain and rinse under cold water. Set aside.
2. **Prepare Sauce:** In a small bowl, whisk together soy sauce, lime juice, maple syrup, rice vinegar, tamarind paste, and sriracha if using. Set aside.
3. **Stir-Fry Vegetables:** Heat vegetable oil in a large skillet or wok over medium-high heat. Add thinly sliced onion and minced garlic. Stir-fry for 2 minutes until fragrant.
4. **Add Vegetables:** Add julienned carrot, thinly sliced bell pepper, and bean sprouts to the skillet. Stir-fry for another 3-4 minutes until vegetables are tender yet still crisp.
5. **Combine Noodles and Sauce:** Add cooked rice noodles to the skillet. Pour the prepared sauce over the noodles and vegetables. Toss everything together until well combined.
6. **Serve:** Garnish with sliced green onions, chopped peanuts, chopped fresh cilantro, and lime wedges. Enjoy this flavorful vegetable pad thai salad as a satisfying meal!

Nutritional Info: Calories: 300 | Fat: 8g | Carbs: 50g | Protein: 8g

Vegan Japchae Noodles

Prep: 20 mins | Cook: 15 mins | Serves: 4

Ingredients:

- 8 oz sweet potato noodles (dangmyeon)
- 2 tablespoons vegetable oil
- 1 onion, thinly sliced
- 2 cloves garlic, minced
- 1 carrot, julienned
- 1 bell pepper, thinly sliced
- 1 cup spinach
- 1 cup sliced mushrooms
- 2 green onions, sliced
- 2 tablespoons soy sauce
- 1 tablespoon sesame oil
- 1 tablespoon maple syrup
- Toasted sesame seeds for garnish

Instructions:

1. **Cook Sweet Potato Noodles:** Cook sweet potato noodles in a pot of boiling water for 5-7 minutes until tender but still chewy. Drain and rinse under cold water. Set aside.
2. **Stir-Fry Vegetables:** Heat vegetable oil in a large skillet or wok over medium-high heat. Add thinly sliced onion and minced garlic. Stir-fry for 2 minutes until fragrant.

3. Add Vegetables: Add julienned carrot, thinly sliced bell pepper, spinach, and sliced mushrooms to the skillet. Stir-fry for another 3-4 minutes until vegetables are tender yet still crisp.
4. Combine Noodles and Sauce: Add cooked sweet potato noodles to the skillet. Pour soy sauce, sesame oil, and maple syrup over the noodles and vegetables. Toss everything together until well combined.
5. Serve: Garnish with sliced green onions and toasted sesame seeds before serving. Enjoy these delicious vegan japchae noodles as a satisfying and flavorful dish!

Nutritional Info: Calories: 250 | Fat: 6g | Carbs: 45g | Protein: 5g

Asian Slaw

Prep: 15 mins | Cook: 0 mins | Serves: 4

Ingredients:

- 4 cups shredded cabbage (green or purple or a mix)
- 1 cup shredded carrots
- 1 bell pepper, thinly sliced
- 1/2 cup chopped fresh cilantro
- 1/4 cup chopped peanuts
- 2 tablespoons rice vinegar
- 1 tablespoon soy sauce
- 1 tablespoon maple syrup
- 1 tablespoon sesame oil
- 1 teaspoon grated ginger
- 1 clove garlic, minced
- Red chili flakes to taste (optional)

Instructions:

1. Prepare Dressing: In a small bowl, whisk together rice vinegar, soy sauce, maple syrup, sesame oil, grated ginger, minced garlic, and red chili flakes if using.
2. Assemble Slaw: In a large bowl, combine shredded cabbage, shredded carrots, thinly sliced bell pepper, and chopped fresh cilantro.
3. Add Dressing: Pour the prepared dressing over the slaw ingredients. Toss gently to coat everything evenly.
4. Chill: Cover the bowl and refrigerate for at least 30 minutes to allow the flavors to meld.
5. Serve: Garnish with chopped peanuts before serving. Enjoy this crunchy and flavorful Asian slaw as a refreshing side dish or light meal!

Nutritional Info: Calories: 150 | Fat: 8g | Carbs: 15g | Protein: 5g

Vegan Sticky Rice

Prep: 5 mins | Cook: 15 mins | Serves: 4

Ingredients:

- 2 cups jasmine rice
- 2 1/2 cups water
- 1/4 cup coconut milk
- 1 tablespoon soy sauce
- 1 tablespoon maple syrup
- 1 teaspoon sesame oil
- 1/4 teaspoon salt
- Toasted sesame seeds for garnish
- Sliced green onions for garnish

Instructions:

1. Rinse Rice: Rinse jasmine rice under cold water until the water runs clear. Drain well.
2. Cook Rice: In a rice cooker or pot, combine rinsed rice and water. Cook according to the rice cooker instructions or bring to a boil, then reduce heat to low, cover, and simmer for 15 minutes until the water is absorbed and the rice is tender.
3. Prepare Seasoning: In a small saucepan, heat coconut milk, soy sauce, maple syrup, sesame oil, and salt until well combined.
4. Mix Seasoning: Once the rice is cooked, fluff it with a fork. Pour the prepared seasoning over the cooked rice and gently mix until well combined.
5. Serve: Garnish with toasted sesame seeds and sliced green onions before serving. Enjoy this sticky and fragrant vegan jasmine rice as a delicious side dish!

Nutritional Info: Calories: 200 | Fat: 5g | Carbs: 35g | Protein: 3g

Steamed Baby Bok Choy

Prep: 5 mins | Cook: 5 mins | Serves: 4

Ingredients:

- 8 baby bok choy, halved lengthwise
- 2 tablespoons soy sauce
- 1 tablespoon rice vinegar
- 1 tablespoon sesame oil
- 1 teaspoon grated ginger
- 1 clove garlic, minced

- Toasted sesame seeds for garnish

Instructions:

1. Prepare Bok Choy: Rinse baby bok choy under cold water and pat dry with a paper towel. Trim the ends and cut in half lengthwise.
2. Prepare Steamer: Fill a steamer pot or a large pot with a steamer basket with water, ensuring it doesn't touch the bottom of the basket. Bring the water to a boil.
3. Steam Bok Choy: Place halved baby bok choy in the steamer basket, cut side down. Cover and steam for 4-5 minutes until tender but still crisp.
4. Prepare Dressing: In a small bowl, whisk together soy sauce, rice vinegar, sesame oil, grated ginger, and minced garlic.
5. Serve: Transfer steamed baby bok choy to a serving platter. Drizzle with the prepared dressing and garnish with toasted sesame seeds before serving. Enjoy these tender and flavorful steamed baby bok choy as a nutritious side dish!

Nutritional Info: Calories: 40 | Fat: 3g | Carbs: 4g | Protein: 2g

Vegan Kimchi

Prep: 30 mins | Cook: 0 mins | Serves: Makes about 2 quarts

Ingredients:

- 1 medium Napa cabbage
- 1/4 cup sea salt
- 4 cups water
- 2 tablespoons grated ginger
- 4 cloves garlic, minced
- 2 tablespoons Korean red pepper flakes (gochugaru)
- 2 tablespoons soy sauce
- 1 tablespoon maple syrup
- 2 green onions, chopped
- 2 carrots, julienned

Instructions:

1. Prepare Cabbage: Cut the Napa cabbage into quarters lengthwise. Remove the core and chop the leaves into bite-sized pieces. Rinse the cabbage under cold water and drain well.
2. Salt Cabbage: In a large bowl, dissolve sea salt in water. Add chopped cabbage and toss to coat evenly. Let it sit for 2 hours, tossing occasionally.

3. **Rinse Cabbage:** After 2 hours, rinse the cabbage under cold water to remove excess salt. Drain well and transfer to a clean, large bowl.
4. **Make Kimchi Paste:** In a small bowl, combine grated ginger, minced garlic, Korean red pepper flakes, soy sauce, and maple syrup. Mix until well combined.
5. **Mix Kimchi:** Add chopped green onions and julienned carrots to the cabbage. Pour the kimchi paste over the vegetables. Using gloves, massage the paste into the cabbage until well coated.
6. **Ferment Kimchi:** Pack the kimchi tightly into clean jars, pressing down to remove air bubbles. Leave about 1 inch of space at the top. Seal the jars loosely.
7. **Fermentation:** Let the jars sit at room temperature for 1-2 days to ferment. Check daily and press down on the kimchi to keep it submerged in its juices.
8. **Store:** Once fermented to your liking, tighten the jar lids and refrigerate. Kimchi will continue to ferment slowly in the refrigerator and can be kept for several weeks.

Nutritional Info: Calories: 30 | Fat: 0g | Carbs: 7g | Protein: 1g

Baked Tofu Teriyaki Bites

Prep: 15mins | Cook: 25 mins | Serves: 4

Ingredients:

- 1 block extra-firm tofu, pressed and cubed
- 1/4 cup soy sauce
- 2 tablespoons maple syrup
- 1 tablespoon rice vinegar
- 1 tablespoon sesame oil
- 1 teaspoon grated ginger
- 2 cloves garlic, minced
- 1 tablespoon cornstarch
- 1 tablespoon water
- Toasted sesame seeds and sliced green onions for garnish

Instructions:

1. **Preheat Oven:** Preheat your oven to 400°F (200°C) and line a baking sheet with parchment paper or lightly grease it.
2. **Prepare Tofu:** In a bowl, whisk together soy sauce, maple syrup, rice vinegar, sesame oil, grated ginger, and minced garlic to make the teriyaki marinade.
3. **Marinate Tofu:** Place the cubed tofu in a shallow dish or a resealable plastic bag. Pour the teriyaki marinade over the tofu, ensuring all pieces are well coated. Let it marinate for at least 15 minutes, or longer for more flavor.

4. Bake Tofu: In a small bowl, mix together cornstarch and water to create a slurry. Dip each marinated tofu cube into the slurry, then place it on the prepared baking sheet. Bake for 20-25 minutes, flipping halfway through, until the tofu is golden and crispy.
5. Serve: Once baked, remove the tofu from the oven and transfer it to a serving plate. Garnish with toasted sesame seeds and sliced green onions. Serve the baked tofu teriyaki bites hot as an appetizer or with rice and vegetables for a complete meal!

Nutritional Info: Calories: 150 | Fat: 7g | Carbs: 12g | Protein: 10g

RICE AND NOODLE DISHES

Vegan Pad Thai

Prep: 15 mins | Cook: 15 mins | Serves: 4

Ingredients:

- 8 oz rice noodles
- 2 tablespoons vegetable oil
- 1 onion, thinly sliced
- 2 cloves garlic, minced
- 1 bell pepper, thinly sliced
- 1 carrot, julienned
- 1 cup bean sprouts
- 1/4 cup chopped peanuts
- 2 green onions, sliced
- Lime wedges for serving
- Chopped fresh cilantro for garnish

For the Sauce:

- 3 tablespoons soy sauce
- 2 tablespoons lime juice
- 2 tablespoons maple syrup
- 1 tablespoon rice vinegar
- 1 tablespoon tamarind paste
- 1 teaspoon sriracha (optional)

Instructions:

1. 1 Cook Rice Noodles: Cook rice noodles according to package instructions. Drain and set aside.
2. Prepare Sauce: In a small bowl, whisk together soy sauce, lime juice, maple syrup, rice vinegar, tamarind paste, and sriracha if using. Set aside.
3. Stir-Fry Vegetables: Heat vegetable oil in a large skillet or wok over medium-high heat. Add thinly sliced onion and minced garlic. Stir-fry for 2 minutes until fragrant.
4. Add Vegetables: Add thinly sliced bell pepper, julienned carrot, and bean sprouts to the skillet. Stir-fry for another 3-4 minutes until vegetables are tender yet still crisp.
5. Combine Noodles and Sauce: Add cooked rice noodles to the skillet. Pour the prepared sauce over the noodles and vegetables. Toss everything together until well combined.

6. Serve: Garnish with chopped peanuts, sliced green onions, and chopped fresh cilantro. Serve with lime wedges on the side. Enjoy this flavorful vegan pad thai as a delicious meal!

Nutritional Info: Calories: 300 | Fat: 8g | Carbs: 50g | Protein: 7g

Vegetable Lo Mein

Prep: 10 mins | Cook: 15 mins | Serves: 4

Ingredients:

- 8 oz lo mein noodles
- 2 tablespoons vegetable oil
- 1 onion, thinly sliced
- 2 cloves garlic, minced
- 1 bell pepper, thinly sliced
- 1 carrot, julienned
- 1 cup sliced mushrooms
- 2 cups shredded cabbage
- 1/4 cup soy sauce
- 2 tablespoons hoisin sauce
- 1 tablespoon maple syrup
- 1 tablespoon sesame oil
- 1 teaspoon grated ginger
- 2 green onions, sliced

Instructions:

1. Cook Lo Mein Noodles: Cook lo mein noodles according to package instructions. Drain and set aside.
2. Stir-Fry Vegetables: Heat vegetable oil in a large skillet or wok over medium-high heat. Add thinly sliced onion and minced garlic. Stir-fry for 2 minutes until fragrant.
3. Add Vegetables: Add thinly sliced bell pepper, julienned carrot, sliced mushrooms, and shredded cabbage to the skillet. Stir-fry for another 3-4 minutes until vegetables are tender yet still crisp.
4. Prepare Sauce: In a small bowl, whisk together soy sauce, hoisin sauce, maple syrup, sesame oil, and grated ginger.
5. Combine Noodles and Sauce: Add cooked lo mein noodles to the skillet. Pour the prepared sauce over the noodles and vegetables. Toss everything together until well combined.

6. Serve: Garnish with sliced green onions before serving. Enjoy this easy vegetable lo mein as a satisfying and flavorful dish!

Nutritional Info: Calories: 280 | Fat: 7g | Carbs: 45g | Protein: 6g

Vegan Fried Rice

Prep: 10 mins | Cook: 15 mins | Serves: 4

Ingredients:

- 2 cups cooked rice (preferably day-old)
- 2 tablespoons vegetable oil
- 1 onion, diced
- 2 cloves garlic, minced
- 1 carrot, diced
- 1 cup frozen peas and carrots, thawed
- 2 tablespoons soy sauce
- 1 tablespoon sesame oil
- 1/4 cup chopped green onions
- 2 tablespoons chopped cilantro (optional)
- Sesame seeds for garnish

Instructions:

1. Heat Oil: Heat vegetable oil in a large skillet or wok over medium-high heat.
2. Sauté Aromatics: Add diced onion and minced garlic to the skillet. Sauté for 2 minutes until fragrant.
3. Add Vegetables: Add diced carrot and thawed frozen peas and carrots to the skillet. Cook for another 3-4 minutes until vegetables are tender.
4. Add Rice: Add cooked rice to the skillet. Break up any clumps and stir-fry for 3-4 minutes until heated through.
5. Season: Drizzle soy sauce and sesame oil over the rice. Stir to combine evenly.
6. Finish: Garnish with chopped green onions, chopped cilantro if using, and sesame seeds before serving. Enjoy this classic vegan fried rice as a delicious side dish or main course!

Nutritional Info: Calories: 220 | Fat: 8g | Carbs: 35g | Protein: 5g

Vegan Chow Mein

Prep: 10 mins | Cook: 15 mins | Serves: 4

Ingredients:

- 8 oz chow mein noodles
- 2 tablespoons vegetable oil
- 1 onion, thinly sliced
- 2 cloves garlic, minced
- 1 bell pepper, thinly sliced
- 1 carrot, julienned
- 1 cup shredded cabbage
- 1/4 cup soy sauce
- 2 tablespoons hoisin sauce
- 1 tablespoon maple syrup
- 1 tablespoon sesame oil
- 1 teaspoon grated ginger
- 2 green onions, sliced

Instructions:

1. Cook Chow Mein Noodles: Cook chow mein noodles according to package instructions. Drain and set aside.
2. Stir-Fry Vegetables: Heat vegetable oil in a large skillet or wok over medium-high heat. Add thinly sliced onion and minced garlic. Stir-fry for 2 minutes until fragrant.
3. Add Vegetables: Add thinly sliced bell pepper, julienned carrot, and shredded cabbage to the skillet. Stir-fry for another 3-4 minutes until vegetables are tender yet still crisp.
4. Prepare Sauce: In a small bowl, whisk together soy sauce, hoisin sauce, maple syrup, sesame oil, and grated ginger.
5. Combine Noodles and Sauce: Add cooked chow mein noodles to the skillet. Pour the prepared sauce over the noodles and vegetables. Toss everything together until well combined.
6. Serve: Garnish with sliced green onions before serving. Enjoy this quick and easy vegan chow mein as a delicious meal!

Nutritional Info: Calories: 280 | Fat: 7g | Carbs: 45g | Protein: 6g

Vegan Pho with Rice Noodles

Prep: 15 mins | Cook: 1 hour | Serves: 4

Ingredients:

- 8 cups vegetable broth
- 1 onion, halved
- 2-inch piece of ginger, sliced
- 3 cloves garlic, smashed
- 1 cinnamon stick
- 2 star anise
- 2 tablespoons soy sauce
- 1 tablespoon maple syrup
- 8 oz rice noodles
- 1 cup sliced mushrooms
- 2 cups bean sprouts
- 2 green onions, sliced
- Fresh cilantro and Thai basil for garnish
- Lime wedges for serving
- Sriracha and hoisin sauce for serving

Instructions:

1. Prepare Broth: In a large pot, combine vegetable broth, halved onion, sliced ginger, smashed garlic, cinnamon stick, star anise, soy sauce, and maple syrup. Bring to a simmer over medium heat. Reduce heat to low and let it simmer gently for 45 minutes to 1 hour.
2. Cook Rice Noodles: Cook rice noodles according to package instructions. Drain and set aside.
3. Prepare Toppings: While the broth is simmering, prepare the toppings. Slice mushrooms, bean sprouts, green onions, and gather fresh cilantro and Thai basil leaves.
4. Strain Broth: Once the broth is done simmering, strain it through a fine-mesh sieve to remove the solids. Discard the solids and return the clear broth to the pot. Keep the broth warm over low heat.
5. Assemble Pho: Divide cooked rice noodles among serving bowls. Top with sliced mushrooms and bean sprouts. Ladle the hot broth over the noodles and vegetables.

6. Serve: Garnish with sliced green onions, fresh cilantro, and Thai basil leaves. Serve with lime wedges, sriracha, and hoisin sauce on the side. Enjoy this comforting vegan pho with rice noodles as a nourishing meal!

Nutritional Info: Calories: 200 | Fat: 1g | Carbs: 40g | Protein: 5g

Vegetable Yakisoba

Prep: 15 mins | Cook: 15 mins | Serves: 4

Ingredients:

- 8 oz yakisoba noodles
- 2 tablespoons vegetable oil
- 1 onion, thinly sliced
- 2 cloves garlic, minced
- 1 bell pepper, thinly sliced
- 1 carrot, julienned
- 1 cup shredded cabbage
- 1 cup sliced mushrooms
- 1/4 cup soy sauce
- 2 tablespoons mirin
- 1 tablespoon maple syrup
- 1 tablespoon sesame oil
- 2 green onions, sliced

Instructions:

1. Cook Yakisoba Noodles: Cook yakisoba noodles according to package instructions. Drain and set aside.
2. Stir-Fry Vegetables: Heat vegetable oil in a large skillet or wok over medium-high heat. Add thinly sliced onion and minced garlic. Stir-fry for 2 minutes until fragrant.
3. Add Vegetables: Add thinly sliced bell pepper, julienned carrot, shredded cabbage, and sliced mushrooms to the skillet. Stir-fry for another 3-4 minutes until vegetables are tender yet still crisp.
4. Prepare Sauce: In a small bowl, whisk together soy sauce, mirin, maple syrup, and sesame oil.
5. Combine Noodles and Sauce: Add cooked yakisoba noodles to the skillet. Pour the prepared sauce over the noodles and vegetables. Toss everything together until well combined.
6. Serve: Garnish with sliced green onions before serving. Enjoy this flavorful vegetable yakisoba as a delicious meal!

Nutritional Info: Calories: 250 | Fat: 6g | Carbs: 45g | Protein: 5g

Vegan Pad See Ew

Prep: 15 mins | Cook: 15 mins | Serves: 4

Ingredients:

- 8 oz wide rice noodles
- 2 tablespoons vegetable oil
- 1 onion, thinly sliced
- 2 cloves garlic, minced
- 1 cup broccoli florets
- 1 carrot, sliced
- 1 bell pepper, thinly sliced
- 1 cup sliced mushrooms
- 1/4 cup soy sauce
- 2 tablespoons vegan oyster sauce
- 1 tablespoon maple syrup
- 1 tablespoon sesame oil
- 2 green onions, sliced

Instructions:

1. 1 Cook Rice Noodles: Cook wide rice noodles according to package instructions. Drain and set aside.
2. Stir-Fry Vegetables: Heat vegetable oil in a large skillet or wok over medium-high heat.
3. Sauté Aromatics: Add thinly sliced onion and minced garlic to the skillet. Sauté for 2 minutes until fragrant.
4. Add Vegetables: Add broccoli florets, sliced carrot, thinly sliced bell pepper, and sliced mushrooms to the skillet. Stir-fry for another 3-4 minutes until vegetables are tender yet still crisp.
5. Prepare Sauce: In a small bowl, whisk together soy sauce, vegan oyster sauce, maple syrup, and sesame oil.
6. Combine Noodles and Sauce: Add cooked rice noodles to the skillet. Pour the prepared sauce over the noodles and vegetables. Toss everything together until well combined.
7. Serve: Garnish with sliced green onions before serving. Enjoy this delicious vegan pad see ew as a flavorful meal!

Nutritional Info: Calories: 280 | Fat: 7g | Carbs: 50g | Protein: 5g

Vegetable Singapore Noodles

Prep: 15 mins | Cook: 15 mins | Serves: 4

Ingredients:

- 8 oz rice vermicelli noodles
- 2 tablespoons vegetable oil
- 1 onion, thinly sliced
- 2 cloves garlic, minced
- 1 bell pepper, thinly sliced
- 1 carrot, julienned
- 1 cup shredded cabbage
- 1 cup bean sprouts
- 2 tablespoons soy sauce
- 1 tablespoon curry powder
- 1 tablespoon maple syrup
- 1 tablespoon sesame oil
- 2 green onions, sliced
- Lime wedges for serving

Instructions:

1. Cook Vermicelli Noodles: Cook rice vermicelli noodles according to package instructions. Drain and set aside.
2. Stir-Fry Aromatics: Heat vegetable oil in a large skillet or wok over medium-high heat. Add thinly sliced onion and minced garlic. Stir-fry for 2 minutes until fragrant.
3. Add Vegetables: Add thinly sliced bell pepper, julienned carrot, shredded cabbage, and bean sprouts to the skillet. Stir-fry for another 3-4 minutes until vegetables are tender yet still crisp.
4. Prepare Sauce: In a small bowl, whisk together soy sauce, curry powder, maple syrup, and sesame oil.
5. Combine Noodles and Sauce: Add cooked rice vermicelli noodles to the skillet. Pour the prepared sauce over the noodles and vegetables. Toss everything together until well combined.
6. Serve: Garnish with sliced green onions and serve with lime wedges on the side. Enjoy these tasty vegetable Singapore noodles as a delightful meal!

Nutritional Info: Calories: 250 | Fat: 6g | Carbs: 45g | Protein: 5g

Vegan Japchae

Prep: 20 mins | Cook: 15 mins | Serves: 4

Ingredients:

- 8 oz sweet potato noodles (dangmyeon)
- 2 tablespoons vegetable oil
- 1 onion, thinly sliced
- 2 cloves garlic, minced
- 1 carrot, julienned
- 1 bell pepper, thinly sliced
- 1 cup spinach
- 1 cup sliced mushrooms
- 2 green onions, sliced
- 2 tablespoons soy sauce
- 1 tablespoon sesame oil
- 1 tablespoon maple syrup
- Toasted sesame seeds for garnish

Instructions:

1. Cook Sweet Potato Noodles: Cook sweet potato noodles in a pot of boiling water for 5-7 minutes until tender but still chewy. Drain and set aside.
2. Stir-Fry Aromatics: Heat vegetable oil in a large skillet or wok over medium-high heat. Add thinly sliced onion and minced garlic. Stir-fry for 2 minutes until fragrant.
3. Add Vegetables: Add julienned carrot, thinly sliced bell pepper, spinach, and sliced mushrooms to the skillet. Stir-fry for another 3-4 minutes until vegetables are tender yet still crisp.
4. Combine Noodles and Sauce: Add cooked sweet potato noodles to the skillet. Pour soy sauce, sesame oil, and maple syrup over the noodles and vegetables. Toss everything together until well combined.
5. Serve: Garnish with sliced green onions and toasted sesame seeds before serving. Enjoy this flavorful vegan japchae as a delicious meal!

Nutritional Info: Calories: 250 | Fat: 6g | Carbs: 45g | Protein: 5g

Vegan Drunken Noodles

Prep: 20 mins | Cook: 15 mins | Serves: 4

Ingredients:

- 8 oz wide rice noodles
- 2 tablespoons vegetable oil
- 1 onion, thinly sliced
- 2 cloves garlic, minced
- 1 bell pepper, thinly sliced
- 1 carrot, julienned
- 1 cup sliced mushrooms
- 1 cup broccoli florets
- 2 green onions, sliced
- 1/4 cup soy sauce
- 2 tablespoons rice vinegar
- 1 tablespoon maple syrup
- 1 tablespoon sriracha (adjust to taste)
- Fresh basil leaves for garnish

Instructions:

1. Cook Rice Noodles: Cook wide rice noodles according to package instructions. Drain and set aside.
2. Stir-Fry Aromatics: Heat vegetable oil in a large skillet or wok over medium-high heat. Add
1. thinly sliced onion and minced garlic. Stir-fry for 2 minutes until fragrant.
2. Add Vegetables: Add thinly sliced bell pepper, julienned carrot, sliced mushrooms, and broccoli florets to the skillet. Stir-fry for another 3-4 minutes until vegetables are tender yet still crisp.
3. Prepare Sauce: In a small bowl, whisk together soy sauce, rice vinegar, maple syrup, and sriracha.
4. Combine Noodles and Sauce: Add cooked rice noodles to the skillet. Pour the prepared sauce over the noodles and vegetables. Toss everything together until well combined.
5. Serve: Garnish with sliced green onions and fresh basil leaves before serving. Enjoy these spicy vegan drunken noodles as a flavorful meal!

Nutritional Info: Calories: 270 | Fat: 6g | Carbs: 50g | Protein: 5g

Vegan Laksa

Prep: 20 mins | Cook: 25 mins | Serves: 4

Ingredients:

- 8 oz rice noodles
- 2 tablespoons vegetable oil
- 1 onion, chopped
- 2 cloves garlic, minced
- 2 tablespoons laksa paste
- 4 cups vegetable broth
- 1 can (14 oz) coconut milk
- 1 tablespoon soy sauce
- 1 tablespoon maple syrup
- 1 cup sliced mushrooms
- 1 bell pepper, thinly sliced
- 1 cup bean sprouts
- 2 green onions, sliced
- Fresh cilantro for garnish
- Lime wedges for serving
- Sriracha for serving (optional)

Instructions:

1. 1 Cook Rice Noodles: Cook rice noodles according to package instructions. Drain and set aside.
2. Sauté Aromatics: Heat vegetable oil in a large pot over medium heat. Add chopped onion and minced garlic. Sauté for 2-3 minutes until softened.
3. Add Laksa Paste: Stir in laksa paste and cook for another 1-2 minutes until fragrant.
4. Prepare Broth: Pour in vegetable broth and coconut milk. Add soy sauce and maple syrup. Bring to a simmer and let it cook for 10 minutes.
5. Add Vegetables: Add sliced mushrooms, thinly sliced bell pepper, and bean sprouts to the pot. Simmer for an additional 5 minutes until vegetables are tender.
6. Serve: Divide cooked rice noodles among serving bowls. Ladle the hot laksa soup over the noodles and vegetables. Garnish with sliced green onions and fresh cilantro. Serve with lime wedges and sriracha on the side. Enjoy this creamy vegan laksa as a comforting meal!

Nutritional Info: Calories: 350 | Fat: 15g | Carbs: 45g | Protein: 8g

Vegetable Chow Fun

Prep: 15 mins | Cook: 15 mins | Serves: 4

Ingredients:

- 8 oz wide rice noodles
- 2 tablespoons vegetable oil
- 1 onion, thinly sliced
- 2 cloves garlic, minced
- 1 bell pepper, thinly sliced
- 1 cup sliced mushrooms
- 2 cups bean sprouts
- 2 tablespoons soy sauce
- 1 tablespoon hoisin sauce
- 1 tablespoon sesame oil
- 2 green onions, sliced
- Toasted sesame seeds for garnish

Instructions:

1. Cook Rice Noodles: Cook wide rice noodles according to package instructions. Drain and set aside.
2. Stir-Fry Aromatics: Heat vegetable oil in a large skillet or wok over medium-high heat. Add thinly sliced onion and minced garlic. Stir-fry for 2 minutes until fragrant.
3. Add Vegetables: Add thinly sliced bell pepper, sliced mushrooms, and bean sprouts to the skillet. Stir-fry for another 3-4 minutes until vegetables are tender yet still crisp.
4. Prepare Sauce: In a small bowl, whisk together soy sauce, hoisin sauce, and sesame oil.
5. Combine Noodles and Sauce: Add cooked rice noodles to the skillet. Pour the prepared sauce over the noodles and vegetables. Toss everything together until well combined.
6. Serve: Garnish with sliced green onions and toasted sesame seeds before serving. Enjoy this flavorful vegetable chow fun as a delicious meal!

Nutritional Info: Calories: 280 | Fat: 8g | Carbs: 45g | Protein: 6g

Vegan Kake Soba

Prep: 15 mins | Cook: 20 mins | Serves: 4

Ingredients:

- 8 oz soba noodles
- 4 cups vegetable broth
- 1 onion, thinly sliced
- 2 cloves garlic, minced
- 1-inch piece of ginger, sliced
- 2 tablespoons soy sauce
- 1 tablespoon mirin
- 1 tablespoon maple syrup
- 1 cup sliced mushrooms
- 2 cups baby spinach
- 2 green onions, sliced
- Nori strips for garnish
- Toasted sesame seeds for garnish

Instructions:

1. Cook Soba Noodles: Cook soba noodles according to package instructions. Drain and set aside.
2. Prepare Broth: In a large pot, bring vegetable broth to a simmer over medium heat.
3. Sauté Aromatics: Meanwhile, heat a small amount of vegetable oil in a skillet over medium heat. Add thinly sliced onion, minced garlic, and sliced ginger. Sauté for 2-3 minutes until fragrant.
4. Add Aromatics to Broth: Transfer the sautéed aromatics to the pot of simmering broth.
5. Season Broth: Stir in soy sauce, mirin, and maple syrup. Let the broth simmer for 10 minutes to infuse the flavors.
6. Add Vegetables and Noodles: Add sliced mushrooms and baby spinach to the pot. Simmer for another 5 minutes until vegetables are tender. Add cooked soba noodles to the pot and heat through.
7. Serve: Ladle the hot kake soba soup into serving bowls. Garnish with sliced green onions, nori strips, and toasted sesame seeds. Enjoy this hearty vegan kake soba as a comforting soup!

Nutritional Info: Calories: 280 | Fat: 5g | Carbs: 50g | Protein: 9g

Vegetable Bibimbap

Prep: 20 mins | Cook: 20 mins | Serves: 4

Ingredients:

- 2 cups cooked white rice
- 2 tablespoons vegetable oil
- 1 carrot, julienned
- 1 zucchini, julienned
- 2 cups spinach
- 1 cup bean sprouts
- 1 cup sliced mushrooms
- 4 tablespoons gochujang (Korean chili paste)
- 4 teaspoons sesame oil
- 4 teaspoons soy sauce
- 2 cloves garlic, minced
- 4 fried or poached eggs (optional)
- 2 green onions, sliced
- Toasted sesame seeds for garnish

Instructions:

1. Cook White Rice: Prepare 2 cups of cooked white rice according to package instructions. Keep warm.
2. Prepare Vegetables: Heat vegetable oil in a large skillet over medium heat. Sauté julienned carrot and zucchini separately until tender. Remove from the skillet and set aside.
3. Sauté Spinach: In the same skillet, add spinach and cook until wilted. Remove from the skillet and set aside.
4. Blanch Bean Sprouts: Blanch bean sprouts in boiling water for 1-2 minutes. Drain and set aside.
5. Sauté Mushrooms: In the same skillet, sauté slicedmushrooms until golden brown and cooked through. Remove from the skillet and set aside.
6. Prepare Bibimbap Sauce: In a small bowl, mix gochujang, sesame oil, soy sauce, and minced garlic to make the bibimbap sauce.
7. Assemble Bibimbap Bowls: Divide the cooked rice among serving bowls. Arrange the sautéed vegetables and mushrooms on top of the rice.
8. Optional: Add Fried or Poached Eggs: If desired, top each bowl with a fried or poached egg.

9. Drizzle with Bibimbap Sauce: Drizzle the prepared bibimbap sauce over the vegetables and rice in each bowl.
10. Garnish and Serve: Garnish with sliced green onions and toasted sesame seeds before serving. Serve immediately, allowing diners to mix the ingredients together before enjoying this colorful and flavorful vegetable bibimbap bowl!

Nutritional Info: Calories: 300 | Fat: 10g | Carbs: 45g | Protein: 9g

Vegan Pad Kee Mao

Prep: 20 mins | Cook: 15 mins | Serves: 4

Ingredients:

- 8 oz wide rice noodles
- 2 tablespoons vegetable oil
- 1 onion, thinly sliced
- 2 cloves garlic, minced
- 2 Thai chilies, thinly sliced (adjust to taste)
- 1 bell pepper, thinly sliced
- 1 cup sliced mushrooms
- 1 cup broccoli florets
- 2 tablespoons soy sauce
- 1 tablespoon vegan oyster sauce
- 1 tablespoon maple syrup
- 1 tablespoon sriracha (adjust to taste)
- 2 green onions, sliced
- Fresh basil leaves for garnish

Instructions:

1. 1 Cook Rice Noodles: Cook wide rice noodles according to package instructions. Drain and set aside.
2. Stir-Fry Aromatics: Heat vegetable oil in a large skillet or wok over medium-high heat. Add thinly sliced onion, minced garlic, and sliced Thai chilies. Stir-fry for 2 minutes until fragrant.
3. Add Vegetables: Add thinly sliced bell pepper, sliced mushrooms, and broccoli florets to the skillet. Stir-fry for another 3-4 minutes until vegetables are tender yet still crisp.
4. Prepare Sauce: In a small bowl, whisk together soy sauce, vegan oyster sauce, maple syrup, and sriracha.
5. Combine Noodles and Sauce: Add cooked rice noodles to the skillet. Pour the prepared sauce over the noodles and vegetables. Toss everything together until well combined.

6. Serve: Garnish with sliced green onions and fresh basil leaves before serving. Enjoy this spicy vegan pad kee mao as a flavorful meal!

Nutritional Info: Calories: 290 | Fat: 7g | Carbs: 50g | Protein: 6g

STIR-FRIES AND CURRIES

Vegan Thai Red Curry

Prep: 15 mins | Cook: 20 mins | Serves: 4

Ingredients:

- 1 tablespoon vegetable oil
- 1 onion, sliced
- 2 cloves garlic, minced
- 2 tablespoons red curry paste
- 1 can (14 oz / 400 ml) coconut milk
- 2 cups mixed vegetables (bell peppers, broccoli, carrots, snow peas)
- 1 block (14 oz / 400 g) firm tofu, cubed
- 2 tablespoons soy sauce
- 1 tablespoon maple syrup
- Fresh basil leaves for garnish
- Cooked rice or noodles, for serving

Instructions:

1. Sauté Aromatics: Heat vegetable oil in a large skillet or wok over medium heat. Add sliced onion and minced garlic. Sauté for 2 minutes until fragrant.
2. Add Curry Paste: Stir in red curry paste and cook for another minute.
3. Simmer with Coconut Milk: Pour in coconut milk and bring to a simmer.
4. Add Vegetables and Tofu: Add mixed vegetables and cubed tofu to the skillet. Simmer for 10-12 minutes until vegetables are tender and tofu is heated through.
5. Season: Stir in soy sauce and maple syrup. Taste and adjust seasoning if needed.
6. Serve: Garnish with fresh basil leaves and serve hot over cooked rice or noodles. Enjoy this flavorful vegan Thai red curry!

Nutritional Info: Calories: 320 | Fat: 25g | Carbs: 15g | Protein: 12g

Vegetable Chop Suey

Prep: 15 mins | Cook: 10 mins | Serves: 4

Ingredients:

- 1 tablespoon vegetable oil
- 1 onion, sliced
- 2 cloves garlic, minced
- 2 cups mixed vegetables (bell peppers, mushrooms, carrots, cabbage)
- 1 cup bean sprouts
- 1/4 cup soy sauce
- 1 tablespoon cornstarch
- Cooked rice, for serving

Instructions:

1. Sauté Aromatics: Heat vegetable oil in a large skillet or wok over medium heat. Add sliced onion and minced garlic. Sauté for 2 minutes until fragrant.
2. Add Vegetables: Add mixed vegetables and bean sprouts to the skillet. Stir-fry for 5-7 minutes until vegetables are tender yet still crisp.
3. Make Sauce: In a small bowl, whisk together soy sauce and cornstarch.
4. Combine: Pour the sauce over the vegetables in the skillet. Stir well to combine and cook for another 2-3 minutes until the sauce thickens.
5. Serve: Serve hot over cooked rice. Enjoy this quick and easy vegetable chop suey!

Nutritional Info: Calories: 150 | Fat: 6g | Carbs: 20g | Protein: 5g

Vegan Massaman Curry

Prep: 20 mins | Cook: 25 mins | Serves: 4

Ingredients:

- 1 tablespoon vegetable oil
- 1 onion, sliced
- 2 cloves garlic, minced
- 2 tablespoons massaman curry paste
- 1 can (14 oz / 400 ml) coconut milk
- 2 cups mixed vegetables (potatoes, carrots, onions)
- 1 cup cubed tofu
- 1 tablespoon soy sauce
- 1 tablespoon maple syrup
- Roasted peanuts for garnish

- Cooked rice, for serving

Instructions:

1. Sauté Aromatics: Heat vegetable oil in a large skillet or pot over medium heat. Add sliced onion and minced garlic. Sauté for 2 minutes until fragrant.
2. Add Curry Paste: Stir in massaman curry paste and cook for another minute.
3. Simmer with Coconut Milk: Pour in coconut milk and bring to a simmer.
4. Add Vegetables and Tofu: Add mixed vegetables and cubed tofu to the skillet. Simmer for 15-20 minutes until vegetables are tender and tofu is heated through.
5. Season: Stir in soy sauce and maple syrup. Taste and adjust seasoning if needed.
6. Serve: Serve hot over cooked rice, garnished with roasted peanuts. Enjoy this comforting vegan massaman curry!

Nutritional Info: Calories: 350 | Fat: 20g | Carbs: 25g | Protein: 10g

Kung Pao Vegetables

Prep: 15 mins | Cook: 15 mins | Serves: 4

Ingredients:

- 1 tablespoon vegetable oil
- 1 onion, sliced
- 2 cloves garlic, minced
- 1 bell pepper, diced
- 1 cup sliced mushrooms
- 1 cup chopped broccoli
- 1/2 cup roasted peanuts
- 2 tablespoons soy sauce
- 1 tablespoon rice vinegar
- 1 tablespoon maple syrup
- 1 tablespoon cornstarch
- 1 teaspoon sesame oil
- Cooked rice, for serving

Instructions:

1. Sauté Aromatics: Heat vegetable oil in a large skillet or wok over medium heat. Add sliced onion and minced garlic. Sauté for 2 minutes until fragrant.
2. Add Vegetables: Add diced bell pepper, sliced mushrooms, and chopped broccoli to the skillet. Stir-fry for 5-7 minutes until vegetables are tender yet still crisp.
3. Add Peanuts: Stir in roasted peanuts and cook for another minute.

4. Make Sauce: In a small bowl, whisk together soy sauce, rice vinegar, maple syrup, and cornstarch.
5. Combine: Pour the sauce over the vegetables in the skillet. Stir well to combine and cook for another 2-3 minutes until the sauce thickens.
6. Finish: Drizzle sesame oil over the stir-fry and toss to coat evenly.
7. Serve: Serve hot over cooked rice. Enjoy this spicy kung pao vegetables stir-fry!

Nutritional Info: Calories: 280 | Fat: 15g | Carbs: 25g | Protein: 10g

Vegan Thai Green Curry

Prep: 20 mins | Cook: 25 mins | Serves: 4

Ingredients:

- 1 tablespoon vegetable oil
- 1 onion, sliced
- 2 cloves garlic, minced
- 2 tablespoons green curry paste
- 1 can (14 oz / 400 ml) coconut milk
- 2 cups mixed vegetables (zucchini, bell peppers, green beans)
- 1 block (14 oz / 400 g) firm tofu, cubed
- 2 tablespoons soy sauce
- 1 tablespoon lime juice
- Fresh cilantro for garnish
- Cooked rice, for serving

Instructions:

1. Sauté Aromatics: Heat vegetable oil in a large skillet or wok over medium heat. Add sliced onion and minced garlic. Sauté for 2 minutes until fragrant.
2. Add Curry Paste: Stir in green curry paste and cook for another minute.
3. Simmer with Coconut Milk: Pour in coconut milk and bring to a simmer.
4. Add Vegetables and Tofu: Add mixed vegetables and cubed tofu to the skillet. Simmer for 10-12 minutes until vegetables are tender and tofu is heated through.
5. Season: Stir in soy sauce and lime juice. Taste and adjust seasoning if needed.
6. Serve: Garnish with fresh cilantro and serve hot over cooked rice. Enjoy this fragrant vegan Thai green curry!

Nutritional Info: Calories: 310 | Fat: 22g | Carbs: 18g | Protein: 12g

Vegetable Pad Prik King

Prep: 15 mins | Cook: 15 mins | Serves: 4

Ingredients:

- 1 tablespoon vegetable oil
- 1 onion, sliced
- 2 cloves garlic, minced
- 2 tablespoons prik king paste
- 1 cup green beans, trimmed and cut into 1-inch pieces
- 1 cup sliced carrots
- 1 block (14 oz / 400 g) firm tofu, cubed
- 1 tablespoon soy sauce
- 1 tablespoon lime juice
- Fresh basil leaves for garnish
- Cooked rice, for serving

Instructions:

1. Sauté Aromatics: Heat vegetable oil in a large skillet or wok over medium heat. Add sliced onion and minced garlic. Sauté for 2 minutes until fragrant.
2. Add Prik King Paste: Stir in prik king paste and cook for another minute.
3. Add Vegetables and Tofu: Add green beans, carrots, and cubed tofu to the skillet. Stir-fry for 5-7 minutes until vegetables are tender yet still crisp.
4. Season: Stir in soy sauce and lime juice. Taste and adjust seasoning if needed.
5. Serve: Garnish with fresh basil leaves and serve hot over cooked rice. Enjoy this spicy and savory vegetable pad prik king!

Nutritional Info: Calories: 270 | Fat: 15g | Carbs: 22g | Protein: 10g

Vegan Japanese Curry

Prep: 20 mins | Cook: 30 mins | Serves: 4

Ingredients:

- 1 tablespoon vegetable oil
- 1 onion, diced
- 2 cloves garlic, minced
- 2 tablespoons curry powder
- 2 cups vegetable broth
- 1 cup diced potatoes
- 1 cup diced carrots

- 1 cup green peas
- 1 block (14 oz / 400 g) firm tofu, cubed
- 2 tablespoons soy sauce
- 1 tablespoon maple syrup
- Cooked rice, for serving

Instructions:

1. Sauté Aromatics: Heat vegetable oil in a large pot over medium heat. Add diced onion and minced garlic. Sauté for 2 minutes until fragrant.
2. Add Curry Powder: Stir in curry powder and cook for another minute.
3. Simmer with Broth: Pour in vegetable broth and bring to a simmer.
4. Add Vegetables and Tofu: Add potatoes, carrots, green peas, and cubed tofu to the pot. Simmer for 20-25 minutes until vegetables are tender.
5. Season: Stir in soy sauce and maple syrup. Taste and adjust seasoning if needed.
6. Serve: Serve hot over cooked rice. Enjoy this rich and comforting vegan Japanese curry!

Nutritional Info: Calories: 300 | Fat: 10g | Carbs: 40g | Protein: 12g

Vegetable Cashew Stir-Fry

Prep: 15 mins | Cook: 15 mins | Serves: 4

Ingredients:

- 1 tablespoon vegetable oil
- 1 onion, sliced
- 2 cloves garlic, minced
- 1 bell pepper, sliced
- 1 cup snap peas
- 1 cup sliced mushrooms
- 1/2 cup roasted cashews
- 2 tablespoons soy sauce
- 1 tablespoon hoisin sauce
- 1 tablespoon cornstarch
- 1 teaspoon sesame oil
- Cooked rice, for serving

Instructions:

1. Sauté Aromatics: Heat vegetable oil in a large skillet or wok over medium heat. Add sliced onion and minced garlic. Sauté for 2 minutes until fragrant.
2. Add Vegetables: Add bell pepper, snap peas, and sliced mushrooms to the skillet. Stir-fry for 5-7 minutes until vegetables are tender yet still crisp.
3. Add Cashews: Stir in roasted cashews and cook for another minute.
4. Make Sauce: In a small bowl, whisk together soy sauce, hoisin sauce, and cornstarch.
5. Combine: Pour the sauce over the vegetables in the skillet. Stir well to combine and cook for another 2-3 minutes until the sauce thickens.
6. Finish: Drizzle sesame oil over the stir-fry and toss to coat evenly.
7. Serve: Serve hot over cooked rice. Enjoy this crunchy and colorful vegetable cashew stir-fry!

Nutritional Info: Calories: 290 | Fat: 18g | Carbs: 25g | Protein: 8g

Vegan Penang Curry

Prep: 20 mins | Cook: 25 mins | Serves: 4

Ingredients:

- 1 tablespoon vegetable oil
- 1 onion, sliced
- 2 cloves garlic, minced
- 2 tablespoons panang curry paste
- 1 can (14 oz / 400 ml) coconut milk
- 2 cups mixed vegetables (bell peppers, zucchini, green beans)
- 1 block (14 oz / 400 g) firm tofu, cubed
- 2 tablespoons soy sauce
- 1 tablespoon maple syrup
- Fresh basil leaves for garnish
- Cooked rice, for serving

Instructions:

1. Sauté Aromatics: Heat vegetable oil in a large skillet or wok over medium heat. Add sliced onion and minced garlic. Sauté for 2 minutes until fragrant.
2. Add Curry Paste: Stir in panang curry paste and cook for another minute.
3. Simmer with Coconut Milk: Pour in coconut milk and bring to a simmer.
4. Add Vegetables and Tofu: Add mixed vegetables and cubed tofu to the skillet. Simmer for 10-12 minutes until vegetables are tender and tofu is heated through.
5. Season: Stir in soy sauce and maple syrup. Taste and adjust seasoning if needed.

6. Serve: Garnish with fresh basil leaves and serve hot over cooked rice. Enjoy this creamy and spicy vegan panang curry!

Nutritional Info: Calories: 310 | Fat: 22g | Carbs: 18g | Protein: 12g

Tofu and Vegetable Stir-Fry

Prep: 15 mins | Cook: 15 mins | Serves: 4

Ingredients:

- 1 tablespoon vegetable oil
- 1 onion, sliced
- 2 cloves garlic, minced
- 1 bell pepper, sliced
- 1 cup broccoli florets
- 1 cup snap peas
- 1 block (14 oz / 400 g) firm tofu, cubed
- 2 tablespoons soy sauce
- 1 tablespoon hoisin sauce
- 1 tablespoon cornstarch
- 1 teaspoon sesame oil
- Cooked rice, for serving

Instructions:

1. Sauté Aromatics: Heat vegetable oil in a large skillet or wok over medium heat. Add sliced onion and minced garlic. Sauté for 2 minutes until fragrant.
2. Add Vegetables: Add bell pepper, broccoli, and snap peas to the skillet. Stir-fry for 5-7 minutes until vegetables are tender yet still crisp.
3. Add Tofu: Stir in cubed tofu and cook for another 2 minutes.
4. Make Sauce: In a small bowl, whisk together soy sauce, hoisin sauce, and cornstarch.
5. Combine: Pour the sauce over the vegetables and tofu in the skillet. Stir well to combine and cook for another 2-3 minutes until the sauce thickens.
6. Finish: Drizzle sesame oil over the stir-fry and toss to coat evenly.
7. Serve: Serve hot over cooked rice. Enjoy this simple and delicious tofu and vegetable stir-fry!

Nutritional Info: Calories: 250 | Fat: 12g | Carbs: 20g | Protein: 15g

Vegan Rendang Curry

Prep: 20 mins | Cook: 40 mins | Serves: 4

Ingredients:

- 1 tablespoon vegetable oil
- 1 onion, sliced
- 2 cloves garlic, minced
- 2 tablespoons rendang curry paste
- 1 can (14 oz / 400 ml) coconut milk
- 2 cups mixed vegetables (potatoes, carrots, bell peppers)
- 1 block (14 oz / 400 g) tempeh, cubed
- 2 tablespoons soy sauce
- 1 tablespoon coconut sugar
- Fresh cilantro for garnish
- Cooked rice, for serving

Instructions:

1. Sauté Aromatics: Heat vegetable oil in a large pot over medium heat. Add sliced onion and minced garlic. Sauté for 2 minutes until fragrant.
2. Add Curry Paste: Stir in rendang curry paste and cook for another minute.
3. Simmer with Coconut Milk: Pour in coconut milk and bring to a simmer.
4. Add Vegetables and Tempeh: Add mixed vegetables and cubed tempeh to the pot. Simmer for 30-35 minutes until vegetables are tender and tempeh is cooked through.
5. Season: Stir in soy sauce and coconut sugar. Taste and adjust seasoning if needed.
6. Serve: Garnish with fresh cilantro and serve hot over cooked rice. Enjoy this aromatic vegan rendang curry!

Nutritional Info: Calories: 350 | Fat: 20g | Carbs: 30g | Protein: 12g

Vegetable Teriyaki Stir-Fry

Prep: 15 mins | Cook: 15 mins | Serves: 4

Ingredients:

- 1 tablespoon vegetable oil
- 1 onion, sliced
- 2 cloves garlic, minced
- 1 bell pepper, sliced
- 1 cup broccoli florets
- 1 cup sliced mushrooms

- 1/2 cup snap peas
- 2 tablespoons soy sauce
- 2 tablespoons teriyaki sauce
- 1 tablespoon cornstarch
- 1 teaspoon sesame oil
- Cooked rice, for serving

Instructions:

1. Sauté Aromatics: Heat vegetable oil in a large skillet or wok over medium heat. Add sliced onion and minced garlic. Sauté for 2 minutes until fragrant.
2. Add Vegetables: Add bell pepper, broccoli, mushrooms, and snap peas to the skillet. Stir-fry for 5-7 minutes until vegetables are tender yet still crisp.
3. Make Sauce: In a small bowl, whisk together soy sauce, teriyaki sauce, and cornstarch.
4. Combine: Pour the sauce over the vegetables in the skillet. Stir well to combine and cook for another 2-3 minutes until the sauce thickens.
5. Finish: Drizzle sesame oil over the stir-fry and toss to coat evenly.
6. Serve: Serve hot over cooked rice. Enjoy this sweet and savory vegetable teriyaki stir-fry!

Nutritional Info: Calories: 240 | Fat: 8g | Carbs: 30g | Protein: 8g

Vegan Yellow Curry

Prep: 15 mins | Cook: 25 mins | Serves: 4

Ingredients:

- 1 tablespoon vegetable oil
- 1 onion, sliced
- 2 cloves garlic, minced
- 2 tablespoons yellow curry paste
- 1 can (14 oz / 400 ml) coconut milk
- 2 cups mixed vegetables (potatoes, carrots, bell peppers)
- 1 block (14 oz / 400 g) firm tofu, cubed
- 2 tablespoons soy sauce
- 1 tablespoon maple syrup
- Fresh cilantro for garnish
- Cooked rice, for serving

Instructions:

1. Sauté Aromatics: Heat vegetable oil in a large pot over medium heat. Add sliced onion and minced garlic. Sauté for 2 minutes until fragrant.
2. Add Curry Paste: Stir in yellow curry paste and cook for another minute.
3. Simmer with Coconut Milk: Pour in coconut milk and bring to a simmer.
4. Add Vegetables and Tofu: Add mixed vegetables and cubed tofu to the pot. Simmer for 15-20 minutes until vegetables are tender.
5. Season: Stir in soy sauce and maple syrup. Taste and adjust seasoning if needed.
6. Serve: Garnish with fresh cilantro and serve hot over cooked rice. Enjoy this mild and creamy vegan yellow curry!

Nutritional Info: Calories: 320 | Fat: 22g | Carbs: 18g | Protein: 12g

Szechuan Tofu and Vegetable Stir-Fry

Prep: 15 mins | Cook: 15 mins | Serves: 4

Ingredients:

- 1 tablespoon vegetable oil
- 1 onion, sliced
- 2 cloves garlic, minced
- 1 bell pepper, sliced
- 1 cup broccoli florets
- 1 cup snap peas
- 1 block (14 oz / 400 g) firm tofu, cubed
- 2 tablespoons soy sauce
- 1 tablespoon Szechuan sauce
- 1 tablespoon cornstarch
- 1 teaspoon sesame oil
- Cooked rice, for serving

Instructions:

1. Sauté Aromatics: Heat vegetable oil in a large skillet or wok over medium heat. Add sliced onion and minced garlic. Sauté for 2 minutes until fragrant.
2. Add Vegetables: Add bell pepper, broccoli, and snap peas to the skillet. Stir-fry for 5-7 minutes until vegetables are tender yet still crisp.
3. Add Tofu: Stir in cubed tofu and cook for another 2 minutes.
4. Make Sauce: In a small bowl, whisk together soy sauce, Szechuan sauce, and cornstarch.

5. Combine: Pour the sauce over the vegetables and tofu in the skillet. Stir well to combine and cook for another 2-3 minutes until the sauce thickens.
6. Finish: Drizzle sesame oil over the stir-fry and toss to coat evenly.
7. Serve: Serve hot over cooked rice. Enjoy this spicy Szechuan tofu and vegetable stir-fry!

Nutritional Info: Calories: 260 | Fat: 12g | Carbs: 25g | Protein: 12g

Vegan Coconut Curry

Prep: 15 mins | Cook: 25 mins | Serves: 4

Ingredients:

- 1 tablespoon vegetable oil
- 1 onion, sliced
- 2 cloves garlic, minced
- 2 tablespoons curry powder
- 1 can (14 oz / 400 ml) coconut milk
- 2 cups mixed vegetables (bell peppers, carrots, cauliflower)
- 1 block (14 oz / 400 g) firm tofu, cubed
- 2 tablespoons soy sauce
- 1 tablespoon maple syrup
- Fresh cilantro for garnish
- Cooked rice, for serving

Instructions:

1. Sauté Aromatics: Heat vegetable oil in a large pot over medium heat. Add sliced onion and minced garlic. Sauté for 2 minutes until fragrant.
2. Add Curry Powder: Stir in curry powder and cook for another minute.
3. Simmer with Coconut Milk: Pour in coconut milk and bring to a simmer.
4. Add Vegetables and Tofu: Add mixed vegetables and cubed tofu to the pot. Simmer for 15-20 minutes until vegetables are tender.
5. Season: Stir in soy sauce and maple syrup. Taste and adjust seasoning if needed.
6. Serve: Garnish with fresh cilantro and serve hot over cooked rice. Enjoy this creamy vegan coconut curry!

Nutritional Info: Calories: 320 | Fat: 22g | Carbs: 18g | Protein: 12g

TOFU AND MEAT ALTERNATIVES

Crispy Baked Tofu

Prep: 10 mins | Cook: 30 mins | Serves: 4

Ingredients:

- 1 block (14 oz / 400 g) firm tofu, pressed and cubed
- 2 tablespoons soy sauce
- 1 tablespoon olive oil
- 1 tablespoon cornstarch
- 1 teaspoon garlic powder
- 1 teaspoon onion powder
- 1 teaspoon smoked paprika
- 1/2 teaspoon black pepper

Instructions:

1. Preheat Oven: Preheat your oven to 400°F (200°C).
2. Prep Tofu: Press the tofu to remove excess moisture, then cut it into 1-inch cubes.
3. Season Tofu: In a large bowl, toss the tofu cubes with soy sauce, olive oil, cornstarch, garlic powder, onion powder, smoked paprika, and black pepper.
4. Bake Tofu: Spread the seasoned tofu cubes on a baking sheet lined with parchment paper. Bake for 25-30 minutes, flipping halfway through, until crispy and golden.
5. Serve: Serve hot with your favorite dipping sauce or over a bed of rice.

Nutritional Info: Calories: 180 | Fat: 9g | Carbs: 10g | Protein: 15g

Vegan "Beef" and Broccoli

Prep: 15 mins | Cook: 15 mins | Serves: 4

Ingredients:

- 1 cup (250 g) vegan beef strips or seitan
- 2 cups (300 g) broccoli florets
- 2 tablespoons vegetable oil
- 1 onion, sliced
- 2 cloves garlic, minced
- 2 tablespoons soy sauce
- 1 tablespoon hoisin sauce
- 1 tablespoon cornstarch mixed with 1/4 cup (60 ml) water

- 1 teaspoon sesame oil
- Cooked rice, for serving

Instructions:

1. Prep Ingredients: Slice the onion and mince the garlic. Mix the cornstarch with water to make a slurry.
2. Cook Vegan Beef: Heat 1 tablespoon of vegetable oil in a large skillet over medium heat. Add the vegan beef strips and cook until browned. Remove and set aside.
3. Sauté Aromatics: In the same skillet, add the remaining oil, onion, and garlic. Sauté for 2-3 minutes until fragrant.
4. Add Broccoli: Add the broccoli florets and stir-fry for 5 minutes until tender-crisp.
5. Combine: Return the vegan beef to the skillet. Add soy sauce, hoisin sauce, and the cornstarch slurry. Cook for another 2-3 minutes until the sauce thickens.
6. Finish: Drizzle sesame oil over the dish and toss to coat.
7. Serve: Serve hot over cooked rice.

Nutritional Info: Calories: 220 | Fat: 10g | Carbs: 15g | Protein: 15g

Vegan Mapo Tofu

Prep: 10 mins | Cook: 20 mins | Serves: 4

Ingredients:

- 1 block (14 oz / 400 g) firm tofu, cubed
- 1 cup (250 g) minced mushrooms
- 2 tablespoons vegetable oil
- 2 cloves garlic, minced
- 1 tablespoon ginger, minced
- 2 tablespoons doubanjiang (spicy bean paste)
- 1 tablespoon soy sauce
- 1 cup (240 ml) vegetable broth
- 1 tablespoon cornstarch mixed with 2 tablespoons water
- 1 teaspoon Sichuan peppercorns, ground
- 2 green onions, sliced
- Cooked rice, for serving

Instructions:

1. 1 Prep Ingredients: Mince the garlic and ginger, and slice the green onions. Cube the tofu.
2. Cook Aromatics: Heat vegetable oil in a large skillet or wok over medium heat. Add minced garlic and ginger. Sauté for 1-2 minutes until fragrant.
3. Add Mushrooms: Add minced mushrooms and cook until they release their moisture and start to brown.
4. Add Spices: Stir in doubanjiang and cook for another minute.
5. Simmer: Add soy sauce and vegetable broth. Bring to a simmer.
6. Add Tofu: Gently add the tofu cubes and simmer for 5-7 minutes.
7. Thicken Sauce: Stir in the cornstarch slurry and cook until the sauce thickens.
8. Finish: Sprinkle ground Sichuan peppercorns and sliced green onions over the top.
9. Serve: Serve hot over cooked rice.

Nutritional Info: Calories: 250 | Fat: 14g | Carbs: 15g | Protein: 15g

Vegan "Chicken" Teriyaki

Prep: 15 mins | Cook: 15 mins | Serves: 4

Ingredients:

- 1 cup (250 g) vegan chicken strips
- 1/2 cup (120 ml) teriyaki sauce
- 1 tablespoon vegetable oil
- 1 onion, sliced
- 1 bell pepper, sliced
- 2 cloves garlic, minced
- 1 tablespoon cornstarch mixed with 1/4 cup (60 ml) water
- 1 teaspoon sesame seeds
- Cooked rice, for serving

Instructions:

1. Prep Ingredients: Slice the onion and bell pepper. Mince the garlic.
2. Cook Vegan Chicken: Heat vegetable oil in a large skillet over medium heat. Add the vegan chicken strips and cook until browned. Remove and set aside.
3. Sauté Vegetables: In the same skillet, add onion, bell pepper, and garlic. Sauté for 3-4 minutes until tender.
4. Combine: Return the vegan chicken to the skillet. Pour in teriyaki sauce and stir well.
5. Thicken Sauce: Stir in the cornstarch slurry and cook until the sauce thickens.
6. Finish: Sprinkle sesame seeds over the dish.

7. Serve: Serve hot over cooked rice.

Nutritional Info: Calories: 260 | Fat: 10g | Carbs: 25g | Protein: 15g

Vegetable Tofu Lettuce Wraps

Prep: 20 mins | Cook: 10 mins | Serves: 4

Ingredients:

- 1 block (14 oz / 400 g) firm tofu, crumbled
- 1 cup (250 g) diced vegetables (carrots, bell peppers, mushrooms)
- 2 tablespoons soy sauce
- 1 tablespoon hoisin sauce
- 1 tablespoon vegetable oil
- 2 cloves garlic, minced
- 1 teaspoon ginger, minced
- 1 head butter lettuce, leaves separated
- 2 green onions, sliced
- 1/4 cup (30 g) chopped peanuts

Instructions:

1. Prep Ingredients: Crumble the tofu and dice the vegetables. Mince the garlic and ginger.
2. Cook Tofu: Heat vegetable oil in a large skillet over medium heat. Add crumbled tofu and cook until browned. Remove and set aside.
3. Sauté Vegetables: In the same skillet, add garlic, ginger, and diced vegetables. Sauté for 3-4 minutes until tender.
4. Combine: Return the tofu to the skillet. Stir in soy sauce and hoisin sauce. Cook for another 2-3 minutes.
5. Assemble Wraps: Spoon the tofu mixture into lettuce leaves.
6. Finish: Top with sliced green onions and chopped peanuts.
7. Serve: Serve immediately. Enjoy these fresh and flavorful lettuce wraps!

Nutritional Info: Calories: 200 | Fat: 12g | Carbs: 15g | Protein: 12g

Vegan Lemongrass "Chicken"

Prep: 15 mins | Cook: 15 mins | Serves: 4

Ingredients:

- 1 cup (250 g) vegan chicken strips
- 2 stalks lemongrass, minced
- 1 tablespoon vegetable oil
- 1 onion, sliced
- 2 cloves garlic, minced
- 1 tablespoon soy sauce
- 1 tablespoon hoisin sauce
- 1 teaspoon coconut sugar
- Fresh cilantro for garnish
- Cooked rice, for serving

Instructions:

1. Prep Ingredients: Mince the lemongrass and garlic. Slice the onion.
2. Cook Vegan Chicken: Heat vegetable oil in a large skillet over medium heat. Add the vegan chicken strips and cook until browned. Remove and set aside.
3. Sauté Aromatics: In the same skillet, add onion, garlic, and minced lemongrass. Sauté for 2-3 minutes until fragrant.
4. Combine: Return the vegan chicken to the skillet. Stir in soy sauce, hoisin sauce, and coconut sugar. Cook for another 2-3 minutes.
5. Finish: Garnish with fresh cilantro.
6. Serve: Serve hot over cooked rice.

Nutritional Info: Calories: 230 | Fat: 10g | Carbs: 20g | Protein: 15g

Vegan BBQ "Pork" Bao Buns

Prep: 30 mins | Cook: 15 mins | Serves: 4

Ingredients:

- 2 cups (250 g) all-purpose flour
- 1/4 cup (50 g) sugar
- 1/2 cup (120 ml) warm water
- 1 teaspoon active dry yeast
- 1 tablespoon vegetable oil
- 1 cup (250 g) vegan BBQ pork
- 2 tablespoons hoisin sauce

- 2 tablespoons soy sauce

Instructions:

1. Make Dough: In a bowl, dissolve sugar in warm water. Add yeast and let sit for 5 minutes until foamy. Mix in flour and vegetable oil to form a dough. Knead for 10 minutes until smooth. Cover and let rise for 1 hour.
2. Prep Filling: While dough rises, mix vegan BBQ pork with hoisin sauce and soy sauce.
3. Shape Buns: Divide dough into 12 portions. Roll each portion into a ball, then flatten and fill with a spoonful of BBQ pork mixture. Pinch to seal and form a bun.
4. Steam Buns: Place buns in a steamer basket and steam for 10-12 minutes until fluffy.
5. Serve: Serve hot. Enjoy these fluffy and flavorful bao buns!

Nutritional Info: Calories: 220 | Fat: 4g | Carbs: 40g | Protein: 8g

Sesame Crusted Tofu

Prep: 15 mins | Cook: 15 mins | Serves: 4

Ingredients:

- 1 block (14 oz / 400 g) firm tofu, sliced into 1/2-inch slabs
- 1/4 cup (30 g) sesame seeds
- 2 tablespoons soy sauce
- 1 tablespoon cornstarch
- 1/4 cup (60 ml) water
- 2 tablespoons vegetable oil
- 2 green onions, sliced

Instructions:

1. Prep Tofu: Slice the tofu into slabs. Mix soy sauce, cornstarch, and water to form a marinade. Marinate tofu for 10 minutes.
2. Coat Tofu: Spread sesame seeds on a plate. Press tofu slabs into sesame seeds to coat both sides.
3. Cook Tofu: Heat vegetable oil in a skillet over medium heat. Fry tofu for 3-4 minutes on each side until golden and crispy.
4. Finish: Garnish with sliced green onions.
5. Serve: Serve hot. Enjoy this crunchy sesame crusted tofu!

Nutritional Info: Calories: 220 | Fat: 14g | Carbs: 10g | Protein: 15g

Vegan Mongolian "Beef"

Prep: 15 mins | Cook: 15 mins | Serves: 4

Ingredients:

- 1 cup (250 g) vegan beef strips
- 1/4 cup (60 ml) soy sauce
- 1/4 cup (50 g) brown sugar
- 2 tablespoons vegetable oil
- 2 cloves garlic, minced
- 1 teaspoon ginger, minced
- 2 green onions, sliced
- 1 teaspoon cornstarch mixed with 2 tablespoons water
- Cooked rice, for serving

Instructions:

1. Prep Ingredients: Mince the garlic and ginger. Slice the green onions.
2. Cook Vegan Beef: Heat vegetable oil in a skillet over medium heat. Add vegan beef strips and cook until browned. Remove and set aside.
3. Sauté Aromatics: In the same skillet, add garlic and ginger. Sauté for 1-2 minutes until fragrant.
4. Make Sauce: Add soy sauce and brown sugar to the skillet. Stir well.
5. Combine: Return the vegan beef to the skillet. Add the cornstarch slurry and cook until the sauce thickens.
6. Finish: Sprinkle sliced green onions over the dish.
7. Serve: Serve hot over cooked rice.

Nutritional Info: Calories: 270 | Fat: 12g | Carbs: 20g | Protein: 18g

Vegan Tempeh Rendang

Prep: 20 mins | Cook: 40 mins | Serves: 4

Ingredients:

- 1 block (8 oz / 225 g) tempeh, cubed
- 1 can (14 oz / 400 ml) coconut milk
- 1 tablespoon vegetable oil
- 1 onion, sliced
- 2 cloves garlic, minced
- 1 tablespoon ginger, minced
- 2 tablespoons rendang curry paste

- 1 tablespoon soy sauce
- 1 tablespoon coconut sugar
- Fresh cilantro for garnish
- Cooked rice, for serving

Instructions:

1. Prep Ingredients: Cube the tempeh. Slice the onion. Mince the garlic and ginger.
2. Sauté Aromatics: Heat vegetable oil in a large pot over medium heat. Add sliced onion, minced garlic, and ginger. Sauté for 2-3 minutes until fragrant.
3. Add Curry Paste: Stir in rendang curry paste and cook for another minute.
4. Simmer with Coconut Milk: Pour in coconut milk and bring to a simmer.
5. Add Tempeh: Add cubed tempeh to the pot. Simmer for 30-35 minutes until tender.
6. Season: Stir in soy sauce and coconut sugar. Taste and adjust seasoning if needed.
7. Finish: Garnish with fresh cilantro.
8. Serve: Serve hot over cooked rice.

Nutritional Info: Calories: 320 | Fat: 22g | Carbs: 15g | Protein: 12g

Vegan Seitan Satay

Prep: 15 mins | Cook: 15 mins | Serves: 4

Ingredients:

- 1 lb (450 g) seitan, cut into strips
- 1/4 cup (60 ml) soy sauce
- 2 tablespoons peanut butter
- 1 tablespoon coconut milk
- 2 cloves garlic, minced
- 1 teaspoon ginger, minced
- 1 tablespoon lime juice
- 1 tablespoon vegetable oil
- 1 tablespoon brown sugar
- Wooden skewers, soaked in water

Instructions:

1. Prep Seitan: Cut seitan into strips. In a bowl, mix soy sauce, peanut butter, coconut milk, minced garlic, ginger, lime juice, vegetable oil, and brown sugar to make a marinade.
2. Marinate: Add seitan strips to the marinade and let sit for at least 30 minutes.
3. Skewer Seitan: Thread marinated seitan strips onto soaked wooden skewers.

4. Cook Seitan: Grill or pan-fry skewers over medium heat for 5-7 minutes on each side until browned and cooked through.
5. Serve: Serve hot with peanut sauce and a side of rice or salad.

Nutritional Info: Calories: 290 | Fat: 15g | Carbs: 18g | Protein: 22g

Vegan "Chicken" Tikka Masala

Prep: 20 mins | Cook: 30 mins | Serves: 4

Ingredients:

- 1 cup (250 g) vegan chicken pieces
- 1 cup (240 ml) coconut milk
- 1 onion, diced
- 2 cloves garlic, minced
- 1 tablespoon ginger, minced
- 2 tablespoons vegetable oil
- 1 can (14 oz / 400 g) diced tomatoes
- 2 tablespoons tomato paste
- 1 tablespoon garam masala
- 1 teaspoon turmeric
- 1 teaspoon cumin
- 1 teaspoon paprika
- 1 teaspoon chili powder
- Fresh cilantro for garnish
- Cooked rice, for serving

Instructions:

1. 1 Cook Vegan Chicken: Heat vegetable oil in a large pot over medium heat. Add vegan chicken pieces and cook until browned. Remove and set aside.
2. Sauté Aromatics: In the same pot, add diced onion, minced garlic, and ginger. Sauté for 5 minutes until soft.
3. Add Spices: Add garam masala, turmeric, cumin, paprika, and chili powder. Stir well and cook for another minute.
4. Simmer Sauce: Add diced tomatoes, tomato paste, and coconut milk. Bring to a simmer and cook for 10 minutes.
5. Combine: Return the vegan chicken to the pot and simmer for another 10 minutes.
6. Finish: Garnish with fresh cilantro.
7. Serve: Serve hot over cooked rice.

Nutritional Info: Calories: 350 | Fat: 22g | Carbs: 25g | Protein: 12g

Tofu Katsu Curry

Prep: 20 mins | Cook: 30 mins | Serves: 4

Ingredients:

- 1 block (14 oz / 400 g) firm tofu, sliced into cutlets
- 1 cup (125 g) panko breadcrumbs
- 1/2 cup (60 g) all-purpose flour
- 1/2 cup (120 ml) plant-based milk
- 2 tablespoons vegetable oil
- 1 onion, diced
- 2 carrots, diced
- 2 potatoes, diced
- 1 apple, grated
- 1 tablespoon curry powder
- 2 tablespoons soy sauce
- 2 cups (480 ml) vegetable broth
- Cooked rice, for serving

Instructions:

1. 1 Prep Tofu: Slice tofu into cutlets. Set up a breading station with flour, plant-based milk, and panko breadcrumbs in separate bowls.
2. Bread Tofu: Dip each tofu cutlet in flour, then plant-based milk, and finally coat with panko breadcrumbs.
3. Cook Tofu: Heat vegetable oil in a skillet over medium heat. Fry tofu cutlets for 3-4 minutes on each side until golden and crispy. Remove and set aside.
4. Sauté Vegetables: In a large pot, add diced onion, carrots, and potatoes. Sauté for 5 minutes until soft.
5. Add Apple and Curry Powder: Stir in grated apple and curry powder. Cook for another 2 minutes.
6. Simmer Sauce: Add soy sauce and vegetable broth. Bring to a simmer and cook for 20 minutes until vegetables are tender.
7. Serve: Serve crispy tofu cutlets over cooked rice with curry sauce on top.

Nutritional Info: Calories: 400 | Fat: 18g | Carbs: 45g | Protein: 12g

Vegan "Beef" Pho

Prep: 15 mins | Cook: 45 mins | Serves: 4

Ingredients:

- 1 cup (250 g) vegan beef strips
- 1 onion, halved
- 1 thumb-sized piece of ginger, sliced
- 4 cups (1 liter) vegetable broth
- 2 cups (480 ml) water
- 2 tablespoons soy sauce
- 2 tablespoons hoisin sauce
- 1 cinnamon stick
- 2 star anise
- 4 cloves
- 1 package (8 oz / 225 g) rice noodles
- Fresh basil, cilantro, and mint for garnish
- Bean sprouts, lime wedges, and sliced chili for serving

Instructions:

1. 1 Char Aromatics: Char onion halves and ginger slices in a dry pot over medium heat until blackened.
2. Simmer Broth: Add vegetable broth, water, soy sauce, hoisin sauce, cinnamon stick, star anise, and cloves to the pot. Bring to a boil, then reduce heat and simmer for 30 minutes.
3. Prep Noodles: Cook rice noodles according to package instructions. Drain and set aside.
4. Cook Vegan Beef: In a separate pan, cook vegan beef strips until browned.
5. Strain Broth: Strain the broth to remove solids. Return broth to the pot and keep warm.
6. Assemble Pho: Divide cooked noodles and vegan beef among bowls. Pour hot broth over the top.
7. Finish: Garnish with fresh basil, cilantro, mint, bean sprouts, lime wedges, and sliced chili.
8. Serve: Serve hot and enjoy the aromatic flavors of this vegan pho.

Nutritional Info: Calories: 320 | Fat: 5g | Carbs: 55g | Protein: 12g

Vegan "Chicken" Larb

Prep: 20 mins | Cook: 10 mins | Serves: 4

Ingredients:

- 1 cup (250 g) vegan chicken pieces, crumbled
- 1 tablespoon vegetable oil
- 2 cloves garlic, minced
- 1 tablespoon soy sauce
- 2 tablespoons lime juice
- 1 tablespoon vegan fish sauce
- 1 tablespoon toasted rice powder
- 1 shallot, thinly sliced
- 2 green onions, sliced
- 1/4 cup (30 g) fresh mint leaves, chopped
- 1/4 cup (30 g) fresh cilantro leaves, chopped
- Lettuce leaves, for serving

Instructions:

1. Cook Vegan Chicken: Heat vegetable oil in a skillet over medium heat. Add crumbled vegan chicken and cook until browned.
2. Add Garlic: Add minced garlic and sauté for 1-2 minutes until fragrant.
3. Mix Sauces: In a bowl, combine soy sauce, lime juice, and vegan fish sauce. Pour over the vegan chicken and stir well.
4. Finish: Stir in toasted rice powder, sliced shallot, green onions, mint, and cilantro.
5. Serve: Spoon the larb mixture into lettuce leaves and serve immediately.

Nutritional Info: Calories: 200 | Fat: 10g | Carbs: 15g | Protein: 15g

DESSERTS AND SWEET TREATS

Vegan Mango Sticky Rice

Prep: 10 mins | Cook: 30 mins | Serves: 4

Ingredients:

- 1 cup (200 g) glutinous rice
- 1 1/2 cups (360 ml) water
- 1 1/2 cups (360 ml) coconut milk
- 1/2 cup (100 g) sugar
- 1/2 teaspoon salt
- 2 ripe mangoes, peeled and sliced
- 1 tablespoon toasted sesame seeds

Instructions:

1. Cook Rice: Rinse the glutinous rice under cold water until the water runs clear. Combine the rice and water in a pot. Bring to a boil, then reduce heat to low, cover, and simmer for 20 minutes.
2. Prepare Coconut Sauce: In a saucepan, combine coconut milk, sugar, and salt. Heat over medium heat until the sugar dissolves. Remove from heat.
3. Mix Rice and Coconut Sauce: Once the rice is cooked, remove it from heat. Pour half of the coconut sauce over the rice, cover, and let it sit for 10 minutes.
4. Assemble: Serve the sticky rice with mango slices on top, drizzled with the remaining coconut sauce, and sprinkled with toasted sesame seeds.

Nutritional Info: Calories: 340 | Fat: 15g | Carbs: 52g | Protein: 4g

Coconut Tapioca Pudding

Prep: 10 mins | Cook: 20 mins | Serves: 4

Ingredients:

- 1/2 cup (75 g) small tapioca pearls
- 2 cups (480 ml) water
- 1 can (14 oz / 400 ml) coconut milk
- 1/4 cup (50 g) sugar
- 1 teaspoon vanilla extract
- Fresh fruit for topping

Instructions:

1. Cook Tapioca: In a pot, bring water to a boil. Add tapioca pearls and cook for 10-15 minutes until translucent, stirring occasionally.
2. Prepare Pudding: Drain the tapioca pearls and return them to the pot. Add coconut milk, sugar, and vanilla extract. Cook over medium heat for another 5 minutes, stirring frequently.
3. Serve: Pour the pudding into bowls and let cool. Top with fresh fruit and serve.

Nutritional Info: Calories: 260 | Fat: 15g | Carbs: 30g | Protein: 2g

Vegan Red Bean Soup

Prep: 10 mins | Cook: 1 hour | Serves: 4

Ingredients:

- 1 cup (200 g) adzuki beans, soaked overnight
- 6 cups (1.4 liters) water
- 1/2 cup (100 g) sugar
- 1 teaspoon vanilla extract
- Pinch of salt

Instructions:

1. Cook Beans: Drain soaked adzuki beans and rinse. In a large pot, combine beans and water. Bring to a boil, then reduce heat and simmer for 45 minutes to 1 hour until beans are tender.
2. Sweeten Soup: Add sugar, vanilla extract, and a pinch of salt to the beans. Stir well and cook for another 10 minutes.
3. Serve: Serve hot or chilled, depending on your preference.

Nutritional Info: Calories: 220 | Fat: 1g | Carbs: 48g | Protein: 7g

Lychee Sorbet

Prep: 10 mins | Cook: 0 mins | Serves: 4

Ingredients:

- 2 cans (20 oz / 565 g each) lychees in syrup, drained
- 1/4 cup (50 g) sugar
- 1/4 cup (60 ml) lime juice

Instructions:

1. Blend Ingredients: In a blender, combine drained lychees, sugar, and lime juice. Blend until smooth.
2. Freeze Mixture: Pour the mixture into an ice cream maker and churn according to the manufacturer's instructions. Alternatively, pour into a shallow dish and freeze, stirring every 30 minutes until fully frozen.
3. Serve: Scoop into bowls and serve immediately.

Nutritional Info: Calories: 150 | Fat: 0g | Carbs: 38g | Protein: 1g

Vegan Mochi Ice Cream

Prep: 20 mins | Cook: 10 mins | Serves: 8

Ingredients:

- 1 cup (160 g) glutinous rice flour
- 1/4 cup (50 g) sugar
- 1 cup (240 ml) water
- 1 cup (240 ml) vegan ice cream
- Cornstarch for dusting

Instructions:

1. Prepare Dough: In a microwave-safe bowl, mix glutinous rice flour, sugar, and water. Microwave for 2 minutes, stir, then microwave for another 1-2 minutes until the dough is cooked through.
2. Shape Dough: Dust a clean surface with cornstarch. Turn the dough out onto the surface and roll it out to about 1/4 inch (0.6 cm) thickness. Cut out circles using a cookie cutter.
3. Assemble Mochi: Place a small scoop of vegan ice cream in the center of each dough circle. Fold the edges over the ice cream and pinch to seal. Place mochi seam-side down in a muffin tin lined with plastic wrap.
4. Freeze: Freeze mochi for at least 2 hours before serving.

Nutritional Info: Calories: 120 | Fat: 2g | Carbs: 26g | Protein: 1g

Vegan Thai Tea Popsicles

Prep: 10 mins | Cook: 10 mins | Serves: 6

Ingredients:

- 2 cups (480 ml) water
- 4 tablespoons Thai tea mix
- 1/2 cup (120 ml) coconut milk
- 1/2 cup (100 g) sugar

Instructions:

1. Brew Tea: In a pot, bring water to a boil. Add Thai tea mix and sugar. Stir until sugar dissolves, then simmer for 5 minutes. Strain and let cool.
2. Mix Coconut Milk: Once the tea is cool, mix in the coconut milk.
3. Pour into Molds: Pour the mixture into popsicle molds and insert sticks.
4. Freeze: Freeze for at least 4 hours or until solid.

Nutritional Info: Calories: 110 | Fat: 4g | Carbs: 18g | Protein: 0g

Vegan Matcha Cake

Prep: 15 mins | Cook: 25 mins | Serves: 8

Ingredients:

- 1 1/2 cups (180 g) all-purpose flour
- 1 cup (200 g) sugar
- 1 teaspoon baking powder
- 1/2 teaspoon baking soda
- 1 tablespoon matcha powder
- 1/2 cup (120 ml) vegetable oil
- 1 cup (240 ml) almond milk
- 1 teaspoon vanilla extract
- 1 tablespoon apple cider vinegar

Instructions:

1. Preheat Oven: Preheat your oven to 350°F (175°C). Grease and flour a cake pan.
2. Mix Dry Ingredients: In a large bowl, whisk together flour, sugar, baking powder, baking soda, and matcha powder.
3. Combine Wet Ingredients: In another bowl, mix vegetable oil, almond milk, vanilla extract, and apple cider vinegar.

4. Combine and Bake: Pour the wet ingredients into the dry ingredients and mix until just combined. Pour the batter into the prepared cake pan.
5. Bake: Bake for 25 minutes or until a toothpick inserted into the center comes out clean. Let cool before serving.

Nutritional Info: Calories: 240 | Fat: 12g | Carbs: 31g | Protein: 2g

Coconut Pandan Waffles

Prep: 10 mins | Cook: 20 mins | Serves: 4

Ingredients:

- 1 1/2 cups (180 g) all-purpose flour
- 2 tablespoons sugar
- 1 tablespoon baking powder
- 1/4 teaspoon salt
- 1 cup (240 ml) coconut milk
- 1/2 cup (120 ml) water
- 1/4 cup (60 ml) vegetable oil
- 1 teaspoon pandan extract

Instructions:

1. Preheat Waffle Iron: Preheat your waffle iron according to the manufacturer's instructions.
2. Mix Dry Ingredients: In a large bowl, whisk together flour, sugar, baking powder, and salt.
3. Combine Wet Ingredients: In another bowl, mix coconut milk, water, vegetable oil, and pandan extract.
4. Combine and Cook: Pour the wet ingredients into the dry ingredients and mix until just combined. Pour batter into the preheated waffle iron and cook according to the manufacturer's instructions.
5. Serve: Serve waffles hot with your favorite toppings.

Nutritional Info: Calories: 220 | Fat: 12g | Carbs: 25g | Protein: 3g

Vegan Black Sesame Soup

Prep: 5 mins | Cook: 15 mins | Serves: 4

Ingredients:

- 1/2 cup (70 g) black sesame seeds
- 1/4 cup (50 g) glutinous rice flour
- 3 cups (720 ml) water
- 1/4 cup (50 g) sugar

Instructions:

1. Toast Sesame Seeds: In a dry skillet, toast black sesame seeds over medium heat until fragrant. Let cool.
2. Grind Seeds: Grind toasted sesame seeds into a fine powder using a blender or food processor.
3. Cook Soup: In a pot, whisk together glutinous rice flour and water. Add ground sesame seeds and sugar. Cook over medium heat, stirring constantly, until the mixture thickens, about 10 minutes.
4. Serve: Serve hot.

Nutritional Info: Calories: 200 | Fat: 10g | Carbs: 24g | Protein: 4g

Vegan Green Tea Cheesecake

Prep: 20 mins | Cook: 0 mins | Serves: 8

Ingredients:

- 1 1/2 cups (180 g) graham cracker crumbs
- 1/4 cup (60 ml) coconut oil, melted
- 1 cup (240 ml) coconut cream
- 1 cup (240 g) cashews, soaked overnight
- 1/2 cup (120 ml) maple syrup
- 1 tablespoon matcha powder
- 1 teaspoon vanilla extract
- 1 tablespoon lemon juice

Instructions:

1. Make Crust: In a bowl, mix graham cracker crumbs with melted coconut oil. Press the mixture into the bottom of a springform pan.
2. Blend Filling: In a blender, combine coconut cream, soaked cashews, maple syrup, matcha powder, vanilla extract, and lemon juice. Blend until smooth and creamy.

3. Assemble Cheesecake: Pour the filling over the crust and smooth the top.
4. Chill: Refrigerate for at least 4 hours or until set.
5. Serve: Slice and serve chilled.

Nutritional Info: Calories: 320 | Fat: 22g | Carbs: 26g | Protein: 6g

Pineapple Upside Down Cake

Prep: 15 mins | Cook: 35 mins | Serves: 8

Ingredients:

- 1 can (20 oz / 565 g) pineapple slices, drained
- 1/4 cup (55 g) vegan butter, melted
- 1/2 cup (100 g) brown sugar
- Maraschino cherries, for garnish
- 1 1/2 cups (180 g) all-purpose flour
- 1 cup (200 g) sugar
- 1 teaspoon baking powder
- 1/2 teaspoon baking soda
- 1/4 teaspoon salt
- 1 cup (240 ml) pineapple juice
- 1/3 cup (80 ml) vegetable oil
- 1 tablespoon apple cider vinegar
- 1 teaspoon vanilla extract

Instructions:

1. Prepare Pan: Preheat oven to 350°F (175°C). Grease a 9-inch round cake pan. Arrange pineapple slices in the bottom of the pan and place a maraschino cherry in the center of each slice. Sprinkle brown sugar evenly over the pineapple slices.
2. Make Batter: In a large bowl, whisk together flour, sugar, baking powder, baking soda, and salt. In a separate bowl, mix pineapple juice, vegetable oil, apple cider vinegar, and vanilla extract.
3. Combine and Pour: Pour wet ingredients into dry ingredients and stir until just combined. Pour batter over the pineapple slices in the cake pan.
4. Bake: Bake for 30-35 minutes or until a toothpick inserted into the center comes out clean.
5. Cool and Serve: Allow the cake to cool in the pan for 10 minutes, then invert it onto a serving plate. Serve warm or at room temperature.

Nutritional Info: Calories: 320 | Fat: 12g | Carbs: 52g | Protein: 3g

Vegan Sesame Balls

Prep: 20 mins | Cook: 20 mins | Serves: 6

Ingredients:

- 1 cup (200 g) glutinous rice flour
- 1/4 cup (50 g) sugar
- 1/2 cup (120 ml) water
- 1/2 cup (80 g) red bean paste
- 1/4 cup (30 g) white sesame seeds
- Oil for frying

Instructions:

1. Make Dough: In a bowl, mix glutinous rice flour, sugar, and water until a smooth dough forms.
2. Form Balls: Take a small piece of dough and flatten it into a disc. Place a small amount of red bean paste in the center and wrap the dough around it to form a ball. Roll the ball in sesame seeds until coated.
3. Fry: Heat oil in a deep fryer or pan to 350°F (180°C). Fry sesame balls in batches until golden brown, about 3-4 minutes. Drain on paper towels.
4. Serve: Serve warm as a snack or dessert.

Nutritional Info: Calories: 180 | Fat: 4g | Carbs: 32g | Protein: 3g

Vegan Mooncakes

Prep: 30 mins | Cook: 25 mins | Serves: 8

Ingredients:

- 1 1/2 cups (180 g) all-purpose flour
- 1/2 cup (120 ml) vegetable oil
- 1/2 cup (120 ml) water
- 1/2 cup (100 g) sugar
- 1 tablespoon golden syrup or maple syrup
- 1/2 cup (120 g) red bean paste
- 8 salted vegan egg yolks (optional)
- Mooncake molds

Instructions:

1. Make Dough: In a bowl, mix flour, vegetable oil, water, and sugar until a smooth dough forms. Let it rest for 30 minutes.
2. Divide Dough: Divide the dough into 8 equal portions. Flatten each portion into a circle.
3. Fill and Mold: Place a spoonful of red bean paste in the center of each dough circle. Optionally, place a salted vegan egg yolk on top of the red bean paste. Wrap the dough around the filling and press into a mooncake mold.
4. Bake: Preheat oven to 350°F (175°C). Place mooncakes on a baking sheet lined with parchment paper. Bake for 20-25 minutes or until golden brown.
5. Cool and Serve: Allow mooncakes to cool completely before serving.

Nutritional Info: Calories: 280 | Fat: 12g | Carbs: 38g | Protein: 4g

Vegan Banana Fritters

Prep: 15 mins | Cook: 15 mins | Serves: 4

Ingredients:

- 4 ripe bananas, peeled and sliced
- 1 cup (120 g) all-purpose flour
- 1/4 cup (50 g) sugar
- 1 teaspoon baking powder
- Pinch of salt
- 1/2 cup (120 ml) water
- Oil for frying

Instructions:

1. Prepare Batter: In a bowl, whisk together flour, sugar, baking powder, and salt. Gradually add water, whisking until smooth.
2. Coat Bananas: Dip banana slices into the batter, ensuring they are fully coated.
3. Fry: Heat oil in a deep fryer or pan to 350°F (180°C). Fry banana slices in batches until golden brown, about 2-3 minutes per side. Drain on paper towels.
4. Serve: Serve warm with powdered sugar or your favorite dipping sauce.

Nutritional Info: Calories: 220 | Fat: 2g | Carbs: 48g | Protein: 3g

Tropical Fruit Spring Rolls

Prep: 20 mins | Cook: 0 mins | Serves: 4

Ingredients:

- 8 rice paper wrappers
- 1 ripe mango, thinly sliced
- 1 ripe papaya, thinly sliced
- 1/2 pineapple, thinly sliced
- 1 kiwi, thinly sliced
- Mint leaves
- Sweet chili dipping sauce or coconut yogurt for serving

Instructions:

1. Prepare Ingredients: Prepare all fruit and mint leaves for rolling.
2. Soak Rice Paper: Fill a shallow dish with warm water. Dip one rice paper wrapper into the water for a few seconds until soft and pliable.
3. Fill and Roll: Place a few slices of each fruit and a mint leaf in the center of the rice paper wrapper. Fold the sides of the wrapper over the filling, then roll tightly to enclose.
4. Serve: Repeat with remaining ingredients. Serve spring rolls with sweet chili dipping sauce

BEVERAGES AND SMOOTHIES

Vegan Thai Iced Tea

Prep: 10 mins | Cook: 10 mins | Serves: 2

Ingredients:

- 2 black tea bags
- 2 cups (480 ml) water
- 1/4 cup (50 g) sugar
- 1/4 cup (60 ml) coconut milk
- Ice cubes

Instructions:

1. Brew Tea: In a pot, bring water to a boil. Add tea bags and let steep for 5 minutes.
2. Sweeten Tea: Stir in sugar until dissolved. Let the tea cool to room temperature.
3. Serve: Fill glasses with ice cubes. Pour the sweetened tea over the ice cubes.
4. Add Coconut Milk: Drizzle coconut milk over the top of each glass.
5. Stir and Enjoy: Stir well and enjoy your creamy vegan Thai iced tea!

Nutritional Info: Calories: 60 | Fat: 3g | Carbs: 8g | Protein: 0g

Vegan Thai Iced Coffee

Prep: 10 mins | Cook: 5 mins | Serves: 2

Ingredients:

- 2 cups (480 ml) brewed coffee, cooled
- 1/4 cup (60 ml) coconut milk
- 2 tablespoons (30 g) sugar
- Ice cubes

Instructions:

1. Prepare Coffee: Brew coffee and let it cool to room temperature.
2. Sweeten Coffee: Stir in sugar until dissolved.
3. Serve: Fill glasses with ice cubes. Pour the sweetened coffee over the ice cubes.
4. Add Coconut Milk: Drizzle coconut milk over the top of each glass.
5. Stir and Enjoy: Stir well and indulge in your rich vegan Thai iced coffee!

Nutritional Info: Calories: 40 | Fat: 2g | Carbs: 6g | Protein: 0g

Vegan Bubble Tea

Prep: 10 mins | Cook: 10 mins | Serves: 2

Ingredients:

- 2 black tea bags
- 2 cups (480 ml) water
- 1/4 cup (50 g) tapioca pearls
- 2 tablespoons (30 g) sugar
- 1/4 cup (60 ml) dairy-free milk of choice
- Ice cubes

Instructions:

1. Cook Tapioca Pearls: Boil water in a pot. Add tapioca pearls and cook for 5 minutes or until they float to the surface. Remove from heat, cover, and let sit for another 5 minutes. Rinse under cold water and drain.
2. Brew Tea: In another pot, bring water to a boil. Add tea bags and let steep for 5 minutes. Let it cool to room temperature.
3. Sweeten Tea: Stir in sugar until dissolved.
4. Serve: Divide the cooked tapioca pearls between two glasses. Fill glasses with ice cubes. Pour the sweetened tea over the ice cubes.
5. Add Dairy-Free Milk: Pour dairy-free milk over the top of each glass.
6. Stir and Enjoy: Insert a wide straw, stir well, and enjoy your refreshing vegan bubble tea!

Nutritional Info: Calories: 150 | Fat: 3g | Carbs: 30g | Protein: 1g

Tropical Smoothie

Prep: 5 mins | Cook: 0 mins | Serves: 2

Ingredients:

- 1 ripe banana
- 1 cup (240 ml) pineapple chunks
- 1 cup (240 ml) mango chunks
- 1/2 cup (120 ml) coconut milk
- 1/2 cup (120 ml) orange juice
- Ice cubes

Instructions:

1. Blend Ingredients: In a blender, combine banana, pineapple chunks, mango chunks, coconut milk, and orange juice.
2. Blend Until Smooth: Blend until smooth and creamy.
3. Serve: Pour into glasses over ice cubes.
4. Garnish (Optional): Garnish with additional fruit if desired.
5. Serve Cold: Serve immediately and enjoy your vibrant tropical smoothie!

Nutritional Info: Calories: 200 | Fat: 5g | Carbs: 40g | Protein: 2g

Dragonfruit Lemonade

Prep: 10 mins | Cook: 0 mins | Serves: 2

Ingredients:

- 1 dragonfruit, peeled and cubed
- 1/4 cup (60 ml) lemon juice
- 2 tablespoons (30 g) sugar
- 2 cups (480 ml) water
- Ice cubes

Instructions:

1. Blend Ingredients: In a blender, combine dragonfruit cubes, lemon juice, sugar, and water.
2. Blend Until Smooth: Blend until smooth and well combined.
3. Strain (Optional): Strain the mixture through a fine mesh sieve to remove any pulp.
4. Serve: Pour into glasses over ice cubes.
5. Garnish (Optional): Garnish with lemon slices or dragonfruit cubes if desired.
6. Serve Cold: Serve immediately and enjoy your refreshing dragonfruit lemonade!

Nutritional Info: Calories: 80 | Fat: 0g | Carbs: 20g | Protein: 1g

Vegan Horchata

Prep: 5 mins | Cook: 0 mins | Chill: 2 hours | Serves: 2

Ingredients:

- 1/2 cup (100 g) white rice
- 2 cups (480 ml) water
- 1/4 cup (50 g) sugar
- 1/2 teaspoon ground cinnamon
- 1/2 teaspoon vanilla extract

- Ice cubes

Instructions:

1. Soak Rice: In a bowl, combine rice and water. Let it soak for at least 2 hours, or overnight.
2. Blend Mixture: Transfer the soaked rice and water to a blender. Add sugar, ground cinnamon, and vanilla extract. Blend until smooth.
3. Strain Mixture: Strain the mixture through a fine mesh sieve or cheesecloth to remove any grit.
4. Chill: Refrigerate the horchata until cold.
5. Serve: Pour into glasses over ice cubes.
6. Garnish (Optional): Sprinkle ground cinnamon on top if desired.
7. Serve Cold: Serve immediately and enjoy your creamy vegan horchata!

Nutritional Info: Calories: 100 | Fat: 0g | Carbs: 25g | Protein: 1g

Vegan Taro Milk Tea

Prep: 10 mins |Cook: 10 mins | Serves: 2

Ingredients:

- 2 cups (480 ml) water
- 2 black tea bags
- 1/4 cup (60 g) taro powder
- 1/4 cup (60 ml) dairy-free milk of choice
- 2 tablespoons (30 g) sugar
- Ice cubes

Instructions:

1. Brew Tea: In a pot, bring water to a boil. Add tea bags and let steep for 5 minutes. Remove the tea bags.
2. Prepare Taro Mixture: In a separate bowl, mix taro powder with dairy-free milk until well combined and smooth.
3. Sweeten: Stir in sugar until dissolved.
4. Combine: Pour the brewed tea into a blender. Add the taro mixture.
5. Blend: Blend until the mixture is smooth and frothy.
6. Serve: Fill glasses with ice cubes. Pour the taro milk tea over the ice cubes.
7. Stir and Enjoy: Stir well and savor the creamy vegan taro milk tea!

Nutritional Info: Calories: 120 | Fat: 2g | Carbs: 25g | Protein: 1g

Vegan Soy Milk

Prep: 10 mins (+ soaking time) | Cook: 20 mins | Serves: 4

Ingredients:

- 1 cup (200 g) dried soybeans
- 4 cups (960 ml) water
- 2-3 tablespoons (30-45 g) sugar (optional)

Instructions:

1. Soak Soybeans: Place dried soybeans in a bowl and cover with water. Let them soak overnight or for at least 8 hours.
2. Rinse and Drain: Rinse the soaked soybeans under cold water and drain.
3. Blend: In a blender, combine soaked soybeans and water. Blend until smooth.
4. Strain: Strain the blended mixture through a nut milk bag or fine mesh sieve into a large pot or bowl, squeezing out as much liquid as possible.
5. Cook: Pour the strained liquid into a large pot and bring to a gentle boil over medium heat, stirring frequently. Reduce heat and simmer for 15-20 minutes, stirring occasionally.
6. Sweeten (Optional): Stir in sugar to taste, if desired, during the last few minutes of cooking.
7. Cool: Remove from heat and let the soy milk cool to room temperature.
8. Store: Transfer the soy milk to airtight containers and refrigerate. Shake well before serving.

Nutritional Info: Calories: 70 | Fat: 4g | Carbs: 2g | Protein: 7g

Vegan Matcha Latte

Prep: 5 mins | Cook: 5 mins | Serves: 1

Ingredients:

- 1 teaspoon matcha powder
- 2 tablespoons (30 ml) hot water
- 3/4 cup (180 ml) dairy-free milk of choice
- 1-2 teaspoons (5-10 g) sugar or sweetener of choice (optional)

Instructions:

1. Prepare Matcha Paste: In a small bowl, whisk matcha powder and hot water together until smooth to create a paste.
2. Heat Milk: In a small saucepan, heat dairy-free milk over medium heat until steaming, but not boiling.
3. Mix Latte: Pour the hot milk into a mug. Add the matcha paste.
4. Sweeten (Optional): Stir in sugar or sweetener to taste, if desired.
5. Froth: Use a milk frother to froth the latte until it becomes creamy and frothy.
6. Serve: Enjoy your frothy vegan matcha latte immediately.

Nutritional Info: Calories: 30 | Fat: 2g | Carbs: 3g | Protein: 2g

Vegan Vietnamese Coffee

Prep: 5 mins | Cook: 5 mins | Serves: 1

Ingredients:

- 2 tablespoons (30 g) coarsely ground coffee
- 1 cup (240 ml) hot water
- 2 tablespoons (30 ml) sweetened condensed coconut milk (store-bought or homemade)
- Ice cubes

Instructions:

1. Brew Coffee: In a drip filter or coffee maker, brew the coarsely ground coffee with hot water to make a strong coffee concentrate.
2. Sweeten Condensed Coconut Milk: In a small bowl, mix the sweetened condensed coconut milk until smooth.
3. Serve: Fill a glass with ice cubes. Pour the brewed coffee over the ice cubes.
4. Add Condensed Coconut Milk: Pour the sweetened condensed coconut milk over the coffee.
5. Stir and Enjoy: Stir well and savor your indulgent vegan Vietnamese coffee!

Nutritional Info: Calories: 80 | Fat: 4g | Carbs: 10g | Protein: 1g

Coconut Lime Cooler

Prep: 5 mins | Cook: 0 mins | Serves: 2

Ingredients:

- 1 cup (240 ml) coconut water
- Juice of 2 limes
- 2 tablespoons (30 ml) agave syrup or sweetener of choice
- Ice cubes
- Lime slices for garnish (optional)
- Mint leaves for garnish (optional)

Instructions:

1. Mix Ingredients: In a pitcher, combine coconut water, lime juice, and agave syrup. Stir until well combined.
2. Chill (Optional): For a colder drink, refrigerate the mixture for 30 minutes.
3. Serve: Fill glasses with ice cubes. Pour the coconut lime mixture over the ice cubes.
4. Garnish (Optional): Garnish with lime slices and mint leaves.
5. Stir and Enjoy: Stir well and enjoy your refreshing coconut lime cooler!

Nutritional Info: Calories: 40 | Fat: 0g | Carbs: 10g | Protein: 0g

Vegan Turmeric Latte

Prep: 5 mins | Cook: 5 mins | Serves: 1

Ingredients:

- 1 cup (240 ml) dairy-free milk of choice
- 1 teaspoon ground turmeric
- 1/2 teaspoon ground cinnamon
- 1/4 teaspoon ground ginger
- 1 tablespoon (15 ml) maple syrup or sweetener of choice
- Pinch of black pepper (optional)
- Ground cinnamon for garnish (optional)

Instructions:

1. Heat Milk: In a small saucepan, heat dairy-free milk over medium heat until steaming, but not boiling.
2. Mix Spices: In a mug, mix together ground turmeric, ground cinnamon, ground ginger, and maple syrup.
3. Combine: Pour the hot milk into the mug with the spice mixture.

4. Whisk: Whisk until the spices are well combined and the latte is frothy.
5. Serve: Sprinkle with a pinch of black pepper and ground cinnamon if desired.
6. Enjoy Warm: Enjoy your golden vegan turmeric latte while it's warm!

Nutritional Info: Calories: 80 | Fat: 3g | Carbs: 12g | Protein: 2g

Vegan Ginger Beer

Prep: 10 mins (+ fermenting time) | Cook: 0 mins | Serves: 4

Ingredients:

- 1 cup (200 g) grated fresh ginger
- 1 cup (200 g) sugar
- 4 cups (960 ml) water
- Juice of 2 lemons or limes
- Club soda or sparkling water
- Ice cubes
- Lemon or lime slices for garnish (optional)

Instructions:

1. Prepare Ginger Syrup: In a saucepan, combine grated ginger, sugar, and water. Bring to a boil, then reduce heat and simmer for 5 minutes.
2. Cool: Remove from heat and let the ginger syrup cool to room temperature.
3. Strain: Strain the ginger syrup through a fine mesh sieve or cheesecloth into a large pitcher.
4. Add Citrus Juice: Stir in the lemon or lime juice.
5. Ferment (Optional): Cover the pitcher and let it ferment at room temperature for 24-48 hours for a stronger flavor. Skip this step if you prefer a non-alcoholic version.
6. Serve: Fill glasses with ice cubes. Pour ginger beer syrup over the ice cubes, filling each glass about halfway. Top with club soda or sparkling water.
7. Garnish (Optional): Garnish with lemon or lime slices.
8. Stir and Enjoy: Stir well and enjoy your spicy vegan ginger beer!

Nutritional Info: Calories: 100 | Fat: 0g | Carbs: 26g | Protein: 0g

Vegan Lassi

Prep: 5 mins | Cook: 0 mins | Serves: 2

Ingredients:

- 1 cup (240 ml) dairy-free yogurt
- 1 ripe mango, peeled and diced
- 1/2 cup (120 ml) coconut milk
- 2 tablespoons (30 g) sugar or sweetener of choice
- Pinch of ground cardamom (optional)
- Ice cubes

Instructions:

1. Blend Ingredients: In a blender, combine dairy-free yogurt, diced mango, coconut milk, sugar, and ground cardamom.
2. Blend Until Smooth: Blend until smooth and creamy.
3. Serve: Fill glasses with ice cubes. Pour the mango lassi over the ice cubes.
4. Garnish (Optional): Garnish with a sprinkle of ground cardamom if desired.
5. Stir and Enjoy: Stir well and enjoy your creamy vegan mango lassi!

Nutritional Info: Calories: 180 | Fat: 6g | Carbs: 30g | Protein: 4g

Vegan Salted Lemon Soda

Prep: 5 mins | Cook: 0 mins | Serves: 2

Ingredients:

- Juice of 2 lemons
- 2 cups (480 ml) cold water
- 2 tablespoons (30 ml) agave syrup or sweetener of choice
- 1/4 teaspoon sea salt
- Ice cubes
- Lemon slices for garnish (optional)
- Sprigs of fresh mint for garnish (optional)

Instructions:

1. Mix Ingredients: In a pitcher, combine lemon juice, cold water, agave syrup, and sea salt. Stir until well combined.
2. Sweeten to Taste: Adjust sweetness by adding more agave syrup if desired.
3. Serve Cold: Fill glasses with ice cubes. Pour the salted lemon soda over the ice cubes.
4. Garnish (Optional): Garnish with lemon slices and sprigs of fresh mint.

5. Stir and Enjoy: Stir well and savor the tangy and refreshing flavor of your vegan salted lemon soda!

Nutritional Info: Calories: 40 | Fat: 0g | Carbs: 10g | Protein: 0g

BASICS AND ESSENTIALS

Vegan Fish Sauce

Prep: 5 mins | Cook: 10 mins | Serves: Makes about 1 cup

Ingredients:

- 1/2 cup (120 ml) soy sauce
- 1 tablespoon (15 ml) rice vinegar
- 1 tablespoon (15 ml) agave syrup or maple syrup
- 1/4 teaspoon nori flakes or powdered seaweed
- 1/4 teaspoon garlic powder
- 1/4 teaspoon onion powder

Instructions:

1. Combine Ingredients: In a bowl, mix together soy sauce, rice vinegar, and agave syrup until well combined.
2. Add Flavorings: Stir in nori flakes, garlic powder, and onion powder.
3. Simmer: Transfer the mixture to a small saucepan and bring to a gentle simmer over medium heat.
4. Reduce: Let it simmer for about 5 minutes, stirring occasionally, until slightly reduced and the flavors meld together.
5. Cool: Remove from heat and let the vegan fish sauce cool to room temperature.
6. Store: Transfer to a sterilized bottle or jar with a tight-fitting lid. Store in the refrigerator for up to 2 weeks.

Nutritional Info: Calories: 20 | Fat: 0g | Carbs: 4g | Protein: 1g

Vegan Oyster Sauce

Prep: 5 mins | Cook: 10 mins | Serves: Makes about 3/4 cup

Ingredients:

- 1/2 cup (120 ml) soy sauce
- 1/4 cup (60 ml) water
- 2 tablespoons (30 g) brown sugar
- 1 tablespoon (15 ml) agave syrup or maple syrup
- 1 tablespoon (15 ml) cornstarch
- 1/2 teaspoon mushroom powder or dried mushroom powder
- 1/4 teaspoon garlic powder

- 1/4 teaspoon onion powder

Instructions:

1. Mix Ingredients: In a bowl, whisk together soy sauce, water, brown sugar, and agave syrup until the sugar is dissolved.
2. Thicken: In a small bowl, mix cornstarch with 1 tablespoon of water until smooth to create a slurry.
3. Combine: Pour the cornstarch slurry into the soy sauce mixture and whisk until well combined.
4. Add Flavorings: Stir in mushroom powder, garlic powder, and onion powder.
5. Cook: Transfer the mixture to a small saucepan and bring to a boil over medium heat, stirring constantly.
6. Simmer: Reduce the heat and let it simmer for about 5 minutes, or until the sauce thickens to your desired consistency.
7. Cool: Remove from heat and let the vegan oyster sauce cool to room temperature.
8. Store: Transfer to a sterilized bottle or jar with a tight-fitting lid. Store in the refrigerator for up to 2 weeks.

Nutritional Info: Calories: 30 | Fat: 0g | Carbs: 7g | Protein: 1g

Vegan Hoisin Sauce

Prep: 5 mins | Cook: 10 mins | Serves: Makes about 1 cup

Ingredients:

- 1/4 cup (60 ml) soy sauce
- 2 tablespoons (30 ml) peanut butter
- 2 tablespoons (30 ml) agave syrup or maple syrup
- 1 tablespoon (15 ml) rice vinegar
- 1 teaspoon sesame oil
- 1/2 teaspoon garlic powder
- 1/2 teaspoon onion powder
- Pinch of Chinese five-spice powder

Instructions:

1. Combine Ingredients: In a bowl, whisk together soy sauce, peanut butter, agave syrup, rice vinegar, and sesame oil until smooth.
2. Add Flavorings: Stir in garlic powder, onion powder, and Chinese five-spice powder.
3. Simmer: Transfer the mixture to a small saucepan and bring to a gentle simmer over medium heat.

4. Reduce: Let it simmer for about 5 minutes, stirring occasionally, until slightly thickened and the flavors meld together.
5. Cool: Remove from heat and let the vegan hoisin sauce cool to room temperature.
6. Store: Transfer to a sterilized bottle or jar with a tight-fitting lid. Store in the refrigerator for up to 2 weeks.

Nutritional Info: Calories: 30 | Fat: 2g | Carbs: 4g | Protein: 1g

Homemade Tofu

Prep: 10 mins (+ soaking and setting time) | Cook: 20 mins | Serves: Makes about 1 pound

Ingredients:

- 1 cup (200 g) dried soybeans
- 4 cups (960 ml) water, plus more for soaking
- 2 teaspoons nigari (natural coagulant) or 2 tablespoons lemon juice
- Cheesecloth or tofu press

Instructions:

1. Soak Soybeans: Place dried soybeans in a large bowl and cover with water. Let them soak overnight or for at least 8 hours.
2. Drain: Drain the soaked soybeans and rinse under cold water.
3. Blend: In a blender, combine soaked soybeans and 4 cups of fresh water. Blend until smooth.
4. Strain: Line a large pot with a double layer of cheesecloth. Pour the soy milk into the pot.
5. Heat: Bring the soy milk to a gentle simmer over medium heat, stirring frequently to prevent scorching.
6. Add Coagulant: Dissolve nigari or lemon juice in 1/4 cup of water. Slowly pour it into the simmering soy milk while stirring gently.
7. Curdle: Let the mixture sit undisturbed for 10-15 minutes until it curdles into tofu curds.
8. Drain and Press: Ladle the curds into a tofu press or wrap them in cheesecloth and press under a heavy weight for 30 minutes to 1 hour.
9. Set: Transfer the pressed tofu to a bowl of cold water and let it set for another 30 minutes.
10. Store: Once set, refrigerate the homemade tofu in an airtight container filled with water for up to 3 days.

Nutritional Info: Calories: 70 | Fat: 4g | Carbs: 2g | Protein: 7g

Vegan Chicken Stock

Prep: 10 mins | Cook: 1 hour | Serves: Makes about 8 cups

Ingredients:

- 8 cups (1.9 liters) water
- 2 large carrots, chopped
- 2 celery stalks, chopped
- 1 large onion, chopped
- 4 cloves garlic, smashed
- 1 handful fresh parsley
- 2 bay leaves

Instructions:

1. Combine Ingredients: In a large pot, add water, chopped carrots, celery, onion, smashed garlic cloves, parsley, and bay leaves.
2. Bring to a Boil: Bring the mixture to a boil over high heat.
3. Simmer: Once boiling, reduce the heat to low and let the stock simmer gently for about 1 hour, uncovered.
4. Strain: After simmering, remove the pot from heat and strain the stock through a fine mesh sieve or cheesecloth into a large bowl or container.
5. Cool: Let the vegan chicken stock cool to room temperature.
6. Store or Use: Once cooled, transfer the stock to airtight containers or use immediately in your favorite recipes.

Nutritional Info: Calories: 10 | Fat: 0g | Carbs: 2g | Protein: 0g

Vegan Beef Stock

Prep: 10 mins | Cook: 1 hour | Serves: Makes about 8 cups

Ingredients:

- 8 cups (1.9 liters) water
- 1 large onion, chopped
- 2 large carrots, chopped
- 2 celery stalks, chopped
- 4 cloves garlic, smashed
- 1/2 cup (8 g) dried shiitake mushrooms
- 2 tablespoons (30 ml) soy sauce or tamari
- 2 tablespoons (30 ml) tomato paste
- 1 teaspoon dried thyme

- 1 teaspoon dried rosemary
- 2 bay leaves

Instructions:

1. Combine Ingredients: In a large pot, add water, chopped onion, carrots, celery, smashed garlic cloves, dried shiitake mushrooms, soy sauce, tomato paste, thyme, rosemary, and bay leaves.
2. Bring to a Boil: Bring the mixture to a boil over high heat.
3. Simmer: Once boiling, reduce the heat to low and let the stock simmer gently for about 1 hour, uncovered.
4. Strain: After simmering, remove the pot from heat and strain the stock through a fine mesh sieve or cheesecloth into a large bowl or container.
5. Cool: Let the vegan beef stock cool to room temperature.
6. Store or Use: Once cooled, transfer the stock to airtight containers or use immediately in your favorite recipes.

Nutritional Info: Calories: 10 | Fat: 0g | Carbs: 2g | Protein: 0g

Vegan Dashi

Prep: 5 mins | Cook: 15 mins | Serves: Makes about 4 cups

Ingredients:

- 4 cups (960 ml) water
- 1 large piece kombu (about 4 inches)
- 1/2 cup (10 g) dried bonito flakes (katsuobushi) (optional for a smoky flavor)

Instructions:

1. Prepare Kombu: In a large pot, add water and kombu. Let it soak for at least 30 minutes to extract flavor.
2. Heat: Place the pot over medium heat and gradually bring the water to a gentle simmer.
3. Remove Kombu: Just before the water comes to a boil, remove the kombu from the pot to prevent bitterness.
4. Add Bonito Flakes (Optional): If using, add the dried bonito flakes to the pot and simmer for 1 minute.
5. Strain: Remove the pot from heat and strain the dashi through a fine mesh sieve or cheesecloth into a large bowl or container.
6. Cool: Let the vegan dashi cool to room temperature.

7. Store or Use: Once cooled, transfer the dashi to airtight containers or use immediately in your favorite Japanese dishes.

Nutritional Info: Calories: 5 | Fat: 0g | Carbs: 1g | Protein: 0g

Vegan Kimchi

Prep: 20 mins (+ fermenting time) | Cook: 0 mins | Serves: Makes about 1 quart

Ingredients:

- 1 medium napa cabbage
- 1/4 cup (60 ml) coarse sea salt
- 2 cups (480 ml) water
- 1 tablespoon (15 ml) soy sauce or tamari
- 2 tablespoons (30 g) gochugaru (Korean red pepper flakes)
- 4 cloves garlic, minced
- 1 tablespoon (15 g) grated ginger
- 2 green onions, chopped
- 1 tablespoon (15 ml) agave syrup or sugar

Instructions:

1. Prepare Cabbage: Cut the napa cabbage lengthwise into quarters and remove the core. Chop the cabbage into bite-sized pieces.
2. Brine Cabbage: In a large bowl, dissolve sea salt in water. Add the cabbage pieces, making sure they are fully submerged. Let it sit for 2 hours, turning occasionally.
3. Rinse and Drain: After 2 hours, rinse the cabbage under cold water to remove excess salt. Drain well and return to the bowl.
4. Mix Paste: In a small bowl, mix together soy sauce, gochugaru, minced garlic, grated ginger, chopped green onions, and agave syrup to form a paste.
5. Combine Paste and Cabbage: Add the paste to the drained cabbage and toss until evenly coated.
6. Ferment: Pack the cabbage mixture tightly into a clean glass jar, pressing down firmly to remove air pockets. Leave about 1 inch of space at the top of the jar. Cover the jar loosely with a lid.
7. Ferment (Cont.): Let the kimchi ferment at room temperature for 1 to 5 days, depending on your preference for fermentation. Check the taste daily.
8. Refrigerate: Once the kimchi reaches the desired level of fermentation, seal the jar tightly and refrigerate to slow down the fermentation process.

Nutritional Info: Calories: 10 | Fat: 0g | Carbs: 2g | Protein: 1g

Vegan Sriracha

Prep: 5 mins (+ fermenting time) | Cook: 10 mins | Serves: Makes about 1 cup

Ingredients:

- 1 pound (450 g) red jalapeno peppers, stems removed
- 4 cloves garlic, peeled
- 1/4 cup (60 ml) distilled white vinegar
- 2 tablespoons (30 ml) agave syrup or sugar
- 1 teaspoon salt

Instructions:

1. Blend Peppers and Garlic: In a blender, combine red jalapeno peppers and peeled garlic cloves. Blend until smooth.
2. Cook Mixture: Transfer the pepper-garlic mixture to a small saucepan. Add distilled white vinegar, agave syrup, and salt. Stir to combine.
3. Simmer: Bring the mixture to a simmer over medium heat, stirring occasionally
4. Reduce Heat: Reduce the heat to low and let the mixture simmer for about 5-7 minutes, allowing the flavors to meld together.
5. Cool: Remove the saucepan from heat and let the sriracha cool to room temperature.
6. Blend (Optional): For a smoother consistency, you can blend the cooled mixture again until desired texture is reached.
7. Store: Transfer the sriracha to a sterilized glass jar or bottle with a tight-fitting lid.
8. Refrigerate: Refrigerate the homemade vegan sriracha for up to 2 weeks.

Nutritional Info: Calories: 5 | Fat: 0g | Carbs: 1g | Protein: 0g

Vegan Sweet Chili Sauce

Prep: 5 mins | Cook: 10 mins | Serves: Makes about 1 cup

Ingredients:

- 1/2 cup (120 ml) rice vinegar
- 1/4 cup (60 ml) water
- 1/2 cup (100 g) granulated sugar
- 2 cloves garlic, minced
- 1 tablespoon (15 ml) soy sauce or tamari
- 1 tablespoon (15 ml) lime juice
- 1 tablespoon (15 ml) cornstarch
- 2 tablespoons (30 ml) cold water
- 1 teaspoon red pepper flakes (adjust to taste)

Instructions:

1. Combine Ingredients: In a small saucepan, whisk together rice vinegar, water, granulated sugar, minced garlic, soy sauce, and lime juice.
2. Bring to a Boil: Place the saucepan over medium heat and bring the mixture to a boil, stirring constantly.
3. Simmer: Reduce the heat to low and let the mixture simmer for about 5 minutes, stirring occasionally.
4. Thicken: In a small bowl, mix cornstarch with cold water to create a slurry. Gradually pour the slurry into the saucepan, stirring constantly.
5. Cook (Cont.): Continue to cook the sauce for another 2-3 minutes, or until it thickens to your desired consistency.
6. Adjust Seasoning: Taste the sauce and adjust the sweetness or spiciness as needed. Add more sugar or red pepper flakes if desired.
7. Cool: Remove the saucepan from heat and let the sweet chili sauce cool to room temperature.
8. Store: Transfer the sauce to a sterilized glass jar or bottle with a tight-fitting lid.
9. Refrigerate: Refrigerate the vegan sweet chili sauce for up to 2 weeks.

Nutritional Info: Calories: 40 | Fat: 0g | Carbs: 10g | Protein: 0g

Vegan Peanut Sauce

Prep: 5 mins | Cook: 5 mins | Serves: Makes about 1 cup

Ingredients:

- 1/2 cup (120 ml) creamy peanut butter
- 2 tablespoons (30 ml) soy sauce or tamari
- 2 tablespoons (30 ml) rice vinegar
- 1 tablespoon (15 ml) agave syrup or maple syrup
- 1 clove garlic, minced
- 1 teaspoon grated ginger
- 1/4 cup (60 ml) warm water (adjust for desired consistency)
- Optional: pinch of red pepper flakes for heat

Instructions:

1. Mix Ingredients: In a bowl, whisk together peanut butter, soy sauce, rice vinegar, agave syrup, minced garlic, and grated ginger until well combined.
2. Thin Sauce: Gradually add warm water to the mixture until you reach your desired consistency. Add more water for a thinner sauce.

3. Adjust Seasoning: Taste the sauce and adjust the flavor as needed. Add more soy sauce for saltiness, vinegar for tanginess, or agave syrup for sweetness.
4. Add Heat (Optional): If desired, add a pinch of red pepper flakes for a spicy kick.
5. Serve or Store: Use the peanut sauce immediately as a dip or sauce, or store it in an airtight container in the refrigerator for up to one week.

Nutritional Info: Calories: 80 | Fat: 6g | Carbs: 5g | Protein: 3g

Vegan Thai Curry Paste

Prep: 15 mins | Cook: 0 mins | Serves: Makes about 1 cup

Ingredients:

- 4 dried red chilies, soaked in warm water for 15 minutes
- 2 shallots, peeled and chopped
- 4 cloves garlic, peeled
- 1 thumb-sized piece of galangal or ginger, peeled and chopped
- 1 stalk lemongrass, tough outer layer removed, chopped
- 1 teaspoon ground coriander
- 1 teaspoon ground cumin
- 1/2 teaspoon ground turmeric
- Zest of 1 lime
- 1 tablespoon soy sauce or tamari
- 1 tablespoon agave syrup or maple syrup
- 1 tablespoon vegetable oil

Instructions:

1. Prepare Ingredients: Drain the soaked red chilies and remove the seeds if you prefer a milder paste.
2. Blend: In a blender or food processor, combine the soaked red chilies, shallots, garlic, galangal or ginger, lemongrass, ground coriander, ground cumin, ground turmeric, lime zest, soy sauce, and agave syrup.
3. Blend (Cont.): Blend until a smooth paste forms, adding a splash of water if needed to help with blending.
4. Fry Paste: Heat vegetable oil in a pan over medium heat. Add the curry paste and cook for 5-7 minutes, stirring constantly, until fragrant.
5. Cool: Remove the pan from heat and let the curry paste cool to room temperature.
6. Store: Transfer the curry paste to an airtight container and store it in the refrigerator for up to two weeks, or freeze for longer storage.

Nutritional Info: Calories: 20 | Fat: 1g | Carbs: 3g | Protein: 1g

Vegan Ponzu

Prep: 5 mins | Cook: 5 mins | Serves: Makes about 1 cup

Ingredients:

- 1/2 cup (120 ml) soy sauce or tamari
- 1/4 cup (60 ml) fresh lemon juice
- 1/4 cup (60 ml) fresh lime juice
- 2 tablespoons (30 ml) rice vinegar
- 2 tablespoons (30 ml) mirin (Japanese sweet rice wine) or rice wine vinegar
- 1 tablespoon (15 ml) agave syrup or maple syrup
- 1 teaspoon grated ginger
- 1 clove garlic, minced
- Optional: 1 teaspoon bonito flakes or kombu (for umami flavor)

Instructions:

1. Mix Ingredients: In a bowl, whisk together soy sauce, lemon juice, lime juice, rice vinegar, mirin, agave syrup, grated ginger, and minced garlic until well combined.
2. Infuse Flavors (Optional): For a deeper umami flavor, add bonito flakes or kombu to the mixture. Let it infuse for 5-10 minutes, then strain.
3. Adjust Seasoning: Taste the ponzu sauce and adjust the flavor as needed. Add more citrus juice for tanginess, soy sauce for saltiness, or agave syrup for sweetness.
4. Serve or Store: Use the ponzu sauce immediately as a dipping sauce or marinade, or store it in an airtight container in the refrigerator for up to one week.

Nutritional Info: Calories: 15 | Fat: 0g | Carbs: 3g | Protein: 1g

Vegan Teriyaki Sauce

Prep: 5 mins | Cook: 10 mins | Serves: Makes about 1 cup

Ingredients:

- 1/2 cup (120 ml) soy sauce or tamari
- 1/4 cup (60 ml) water
- 1/4 cup (50 g) brown sugar
- 2 tablespoons (30 ml) rice vinegar
- 2 cloves garlic, minced
- 1 teaspoon grated ginger
- 1 tablespoon (15 ml) agave syrup or maple syrup
- 1 tablespoon (15 ml) cornstarch
- 2 tablespoons (30 ml) cold water

Instructions:

1. Combine Ingredients: In a small saucepan, whisk together soy sauce, water, brown sugar, rice vinegar, minced garlic, grated ginger, and agave syrup.
2. Simmer: Place the saucepan over medium heat and bring the mixture to a simmer, stirring occasionally.
3. Thicken Sauce: In a small bowl, mix cornstarch with cold water to create a slurry. Gradually pour the slurry into the simmering sauce, stirring constantly.
4. Cook (Cont.): Continue to cook the sauce for another 2-3 minutes, or until it thickens to your desired consistency.
5. Adjust Seasoning: Taste the teriyaki sauce and adjust the flavor as needed. Add more soy sauce for saltiness, brown sugar for sweetness, or rice vinegar for tanginess.
6. Serve or Store: Use the teriyaki sauce immediately as a marinade or glaze, or store it in an airtight container in the refrigerator for up to one week.

Nutritional Info: Calories: 50 | Fat: 0g | Carbs: 12g | Protein: 1g

Vegan Gochujang

Prep: 10 mins | Cook: 0 mins | Serves: Makes about 1 cup

Ingredients:

- 1/2 cup (120 g) Korean red chili powder (gochugaru)
- 1/4 cup (60 g) miso paste
- 1/4 cup (60 ml) soy sauce or tamari
- 2 tablespoons (30 ml) rice vinegar
- 2 tablespoons (30 ml) agave syrup or maple syrup
- 4 cloves garlic, minced
- 1 tablespoon grated ginger
- 1 tablespoon toasted sesame oil

Instructions:

1. Combine Ingredients: In a bowl, mix together Korean red chili powder, miso paste, soy sauce, rice vinegar, agave syrup, minced garlic, grated ginger, and toasted sesame oil until well combined.
2. Adjust Consistency: If the gochujang paste is too thick, you can add a tablespoon of water at a time until you reach your desired consistency.
3. Adjust Seasoning: Taste the gochujang paste and adjust the flavor as needed. Add more soy sauce for saltiness, rice vinegar for tanginess, or agave syrup for sweetness.
4. Serve or Store: Use the gochujang paste immediately in your favorite Korean dishes, or store it in an airtight container in the refrigerator for up to one month.

Nutritional Info: Calories: 30 | Fat: 1g | Carbs: 5g | Protein: 1g

CONCLUSION

The Vegan Asian Cookbook offers a delightful exploration into the vibrant and diverse world of plant-based cuisine inspired by Asian flavors. Throughout its pages, this cookbook celebrates the rich tapestry of culinary traditions from across Asia, providing a treasure trove of recipes that are both convenient and delicious. With a focus on convenience, each recipe is crafted to be accessible to home cooks of all skill levels, making it easy to bring the bold and complex flavors of Asian cuisine to your own kitchen.

One of the cookbook's greatest strengths lies in its comprehensive coverage of a wide range of dishes, from appetizers and snacks to main courses, side dishes, desserts, and beverages. Whether you're craving the crispy crunch of spring rolls, the comforting warmth of a bowl of miso soup, or the indulgent sweetness of mango sticky rice, there's something for everyone to enjoy. With each recipe thoughtfully curated and meticulously tested, you can trust that each dish will turn out perfectly every time.

What sets the Vegan Asian Cookbook apart is its commitment to authenticity. While all recipes are entirely plant-based, they stay true to the traditional flavors and techniques of Asian cuisine. From homemade curry pastes and sauces to perfectly cooked noodles and rice dishes, each recipe captures the essence of Asian cooking, allowing you to savor the flavors of the region without compromising on your dietary preferences.

Beyond its culinary offerings, the Vegan Asian Cookbook serves as a gateway to discovering new ingredients and flavors. With detailed explanations of key ingredients and handy tips for navigating Asian markets, this cookbook empowers home cooks to experiment with new flavors and expand their culinary horizons. Whether you're stocking up on pantry staples like soy sauce and rice vinegar or exploring lesser-known ingredients like gochujang and miso paste, you'll find everything you need to create authentic Asian-inspired dishes.

In addition to its focus on authenticity, the Vegan Asian Cookbook also prioritizes convenience and accessibility. With clear, concise instructions and easy-to-follow recipes, even novice cooks can feel confident tackling complex dishes like vegan ramen or Thai curry. Each recipe is accompanied by helpful tips and tricks to ensure success, making it easy to recreate your favorite Asian dishes at home.

Moreover, the Vegan Asian Cookbook recognizes the importance of nutritional balance and transparency. With accurate nutritional information provided for each recipe, you can make informed choices about your meals and ensure they align with your dietary goals. Whether you're looking to boost your protein intake with tofu and tempeh or incorporate more vegetables into your diet with stir-fries and salads, the cookbook provides all the information you need to make healthy choices without sacrificing flavor.

In conclusion, the Vegan Asian Cookbook is a celebration of the rich and diverse culinary heritage of Asia, offering a wide array of plant-based recipes that are as flavorful as they are nourishing. From appetizers and snacks to main courses, side dishes, desserts, and beverages, this cookbook has something for every palate and occasion. With its focus on authenticity, convenience, and nutritional balance, it's the perfect companion for anyone looking to explore the vibrant world of Asian-inspired vegan cooking. So why not embark on a culinary adventure and bring the flavors of Asia into your own kitchen today?

Printed in Great Britain
by Amazon